Marx Hardy Montaigne Machiavelli Chesterton Cooper Emerson Joyce Austen
Defoe Abbott Melville Haggard Hugo Eliot Grimm
Stoker Carroll Christie Moliere Byron Schiller
Wilde Maupassant Engels Smith Kafka Hall Willis
Garnett Einstein Fitzgerald Hawthorne Dostoyevsky
Goethe Cotton Kipling Doyle
Baum Henry Nietzsche
Leslie Dumas Flaubert Turgenev Balzac Crane
Stockton Vatsyayana Verne
Burroughs Gogol Vinci
Curtis Tocqueville Whitman Busch
Homer Widger Tolstoy
Darwin Thoreau Twain Scott Plato Harte
Potter Freud Zola Lawrence Dickens Burton Hesse
Kant Jowett Stevenson
Andersen Cervantes
London Descartes Voltaire
Poe Aristotle Wells Cooke
Hale James Hastings
Bunner Shakespeare Irving
Richter Chekhov Chambers da Shaw Wodehouse Benedict Alcott
Dore Dante Pushkin Newton
Swift

 tredition®

tredition was established in 2006 by Sandra Latusseck and Soenke Schulz. Based in Hamburg, Germany, tredition offers publishing solutions to authors and publishing houses, combined with world-wide distribution of printed and digital book content. tredition is uniquely positioned to enable authors and publishing houses to create books on their own terms and without conventional manufacturing risks.

For more information please visit: www.tredition.com

TREDITION CLASSICS

This book is part of the TREDITION CLASSICS series. The creators of this series are united by passion for literature and driven by the intention of making all public domain books available in printed format again - worldwide. Most TREDITION CLASSICS titles have been out of print and off the bookstore shelves for decades. At tredition we believe that a great book never goes out of style and that its value is eternal. Several mostly non-profit literature projects provide content to tredition. To support their good work, tredition donates a portion of the proceeds from each sold copy. As a reader of a TREDITION CLASSICS book, you support our mission to save many of the amazing works of world literature from oblivion. See all available books at www.tredition.com.

Project Gutenberg

The content for this book has been graciously provided by Project Gutenberg. Project Gutenberg is a non-profit organization founded by Michael Hart in 1971 at the University of Illinois. The mission of Project Gutenberg is simple: To encourage the creation and distribution of eBooks. Project Gutenberg is the first and largest collection of public domain eBooks.

A Guide to Peterborough Cathedral Comprising a brief history of the monastery from its foundation to the present time, with a descriptive account of its architectural peculiarities and recent improvements, compiled from the works of Gunton, Britton, and original & authentic documents

George S. (George Searle) Phillips

Imprint

This book is part of TREDITION CLASSICS

Author: George S. (George Searle) Phillips
Cover design: Buchgut, Berlin – Germany

Publisher: tredition GmbH, Hamburg - Germany
ISBN: 978-3-8472-2995-7

www.tredition.com
www.tredition.de

Copyright:
The content of this book is sourced from the public domain.

The intention of the TREDITION CLASSICS series is to make world literature in the public domain available in printed format. Literary enthusiasts and organizations, such as Project Gutenberg, worldwide have scanned and digitally edited the original texts. tredition has subsequently formatted and redesigned the content into a modern reading layout. Therefore, we cannot guarantee the exact reproduction of the original format of a particular historic edition. Please also note that no modifications have been made to the spelling, therefore it may differ from the orthography used today.

NEW GUIDE

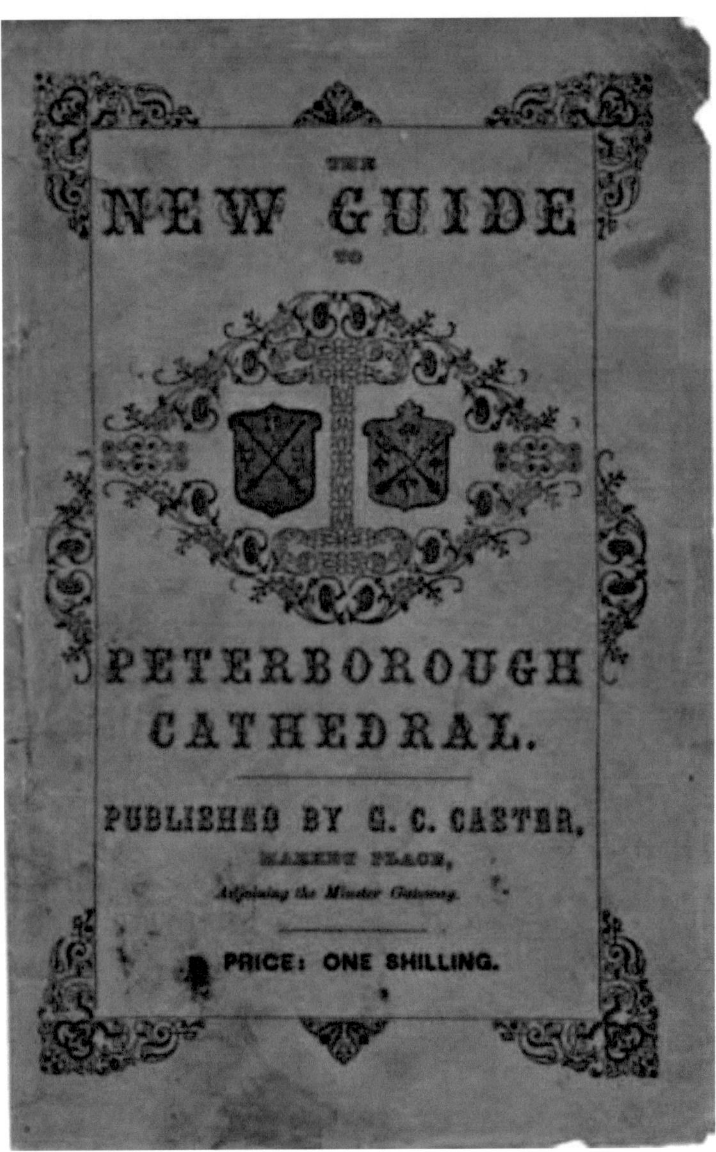

PETERBOROUGH
CATHEDRAL.

PUBLISHED BY G. C. CASTER,

MARKET PLACE,

Adjoining the Minster Gateway.

PRICE: ONE SHILLING.

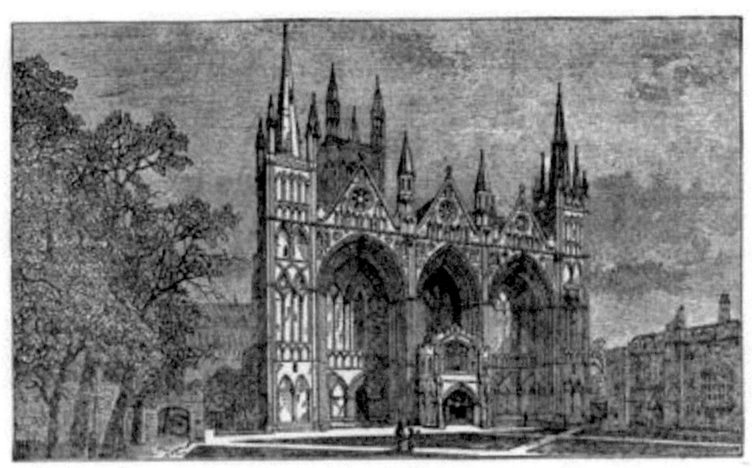

Peterborough Cathedral — West Front

A GUIDE TO PETERBOROUGH CATHEDRAL.

CHAPTER I.

From the foundation of the monastery by Peada, a.d. 655, to its destruction by fire in the reign of Henry the First; — embracing a period of 461 years.

The history of our monastic establishments is but little regarded and as little known. The obscurity in which all monastic institutions is involved renders it difficult to give any certain and positive information respecting the origin of the building to whose history these pages are devoted; but it appears to have been founded at a very early period — the churches of Canterbury, Rochester, London, Westminster, York, and Winchester, being the only large sacred edifices that preceded it. The date of the first building is stated to have been a.d. 655 — fifty-eight years after the introduction of Christianity into England by St. Augustine; and so large were the foundation stones, that it required eight yoke of oxen to draw them. From this it may be inferred that the structure was not, like many of the Anglo-Saxon churches of this period — built entirely of wood; though it was probably far inferior in size and style of architecture to the building which succeeded it.

It was one of the kings of Mercia who laid the foundation of the monastery of *Medeshamstede*[1] in 655; his name was Peada, the eldest son of Penda, the fourth monarch of that kingdom. The facts are thus related by the Saxon chronicler: — "From the beginning of the world had now elapsed 5,850 winters, when Peada the son of Penda assumed the government of the Mercians. In his time came together himself and Osway, brother of King Oswald, and said they would rear a *minster* to the glory of Christ and honour of Saint Peter; and they did so, and gave it the name of *Medeshamstede*, because there is a well there called *Medeswell*. And they began the ground-wall and wrought thereon, after which they committed the work to a monk, whose name was Saxulf. Peada reigned no while, for he was betrayed by his own queen in Eastertide, 658."

Wolfere was the youngest son of Penda, and when Peada died, King Osway assumed the government of Mercia, and ruled very despotically for about three years, when the nobles, incensed at his conduct, rebelled against him, drove him from the kingdom, and chose Wolfere for their king. It was in his reign that "*Medeshamstede* waxed rich," for Wolfere not only caused the monastery to be built, but he endowed it with a great number of lands, and made it "not subject except to Rome alone;" and the abbey, which was by this time completed, was dedicated with great pomp and ceremony to "Christ and St. Peter," and hallowed in the name of "Saint Peter and Saint Andrew."

Saxulf, who had superintended the building of the abbey, was the first abbot whose name is mentioned in the monkish chronicles as its ruler. He was remarkable for his learning, piety, and humility, and was chiefly instrumental in bringing Christianity into the kingdom of Mercia. Both Saxulf and Cuthbaldus who succeeded him were abbots of the monastery during the rule of Wolfere, although there is little mention made of either in the records which have been handed down to us.

Wolfere died in 683, and was succeeded by his brother Ethelred, who contributed very largely to the monastery, and secured to it by his interest extraordinary privileges. Those who could not afford to go to Rome to offer up vows and get absolved from their sins were allowed both indulgences at this monastery, and could likewise receive "the apostolical benediction." Ethelred built a house for the abbot, which is now the palace of the bishop, but, excepting for its antiquity, it possesses no features of interest.

After a reign of thirty years, Ethelred exchanged the insignia of royalty for the rough garments of a monk, and became abbot of Bardney, in Lincolnshire, where he died, in the year, 716.

From the death of Cuthbaldus to the accession of Beonna in 775, there is a blank in the history of the monastery. During his rule one or two important concessions were made to the monks by King Offa.

The name of the next abbot was Celredus, but of him nothing particular is recorded. He was succeeded by Hedda, in 833, during whose abbacy the first destruction of the monastery by the Danes occurred, which founded an important era in the history of this institution. A band of savage Danes, headed by Earl Hubba, invaded the territory of the Mercians, and after committing numerous depredations in the country, they plundered the monastery of Croyland, and proceeded to attack *Medeshamstede*. The monks of this abbey had, however, gained intelligence of their intentions, and having closed the gates, resolved to act on the defensive. Hubba and his desperadoes soon surrounded them, and demanded that the gates should be opened; and when he was told that he should not enter, he commenced to batter the walls. In the course of the attack, one of the monks hurled a great stone from the top of the building upon the besiegers, and Tulba, the brother of Hubba, was killed by it. This so incensed the earl, that he vowed to put every monk to death by his own hand; and having forced the gates, proceeded to put his horrible threat into execution,—robbed the monastery of everything that was valuable, and then set it on fire. It burned fifteen days. All the portable valuables were then packed on waggons and taken away. The plunder, however, is said to have been lost, "either in the Nen or in the neighbouring marshes."[2] This was in 870.

In a short time a few monks who escaped at Croyland re-assembled at their abbey there, and after electing Godric their abbot, proceeded to *Medeshamstede*, and buried the monks of that monastery who had been murdered by the Danish invaders in one vast tomb. Godric likewise had their effigies cut out in stone (a representation of which is here shown, the original being in the Lady Chapel),[3] and, to honour their memory, he went every year to weep over the grave in which he had laid his brethren.

From this time until the reign of Alfred the Great [872] the monastery of *Medeshamstede* was frequently invaded, and the lands which belonged to it were seized by the conquerors. It was left for the wisdom and courage of Alfred to restore that tranquility to England which it had so long lost, and to give protection and security to his subjects. The Danes who had committed so many depredations before his accession to the throne were now beaten back and finally checked by the powerful fleet which he built to protect the kingdom from invasion. King Edgar, who succeeded Alfred, followed his example in this respect, and kept up the strength of the fleet. By this means increased security was given to England, and the people, comparatively happy in their internal government, and freed from the fear of foreign interruption, began to improve their public buildings and religious houses.

It was in 966 that the monastery of *Medeshamstede* was rebuilt after the old model, at the instigation of Athelwold, who was at that time Bishop of Winchester. King Edgar assisted in the reconstruction of the monastery; and so important did he consider religion to be in the amelioration of the morals of his subjects, that he is said to have rebuilt upwards of forty religious establishments during his reign.

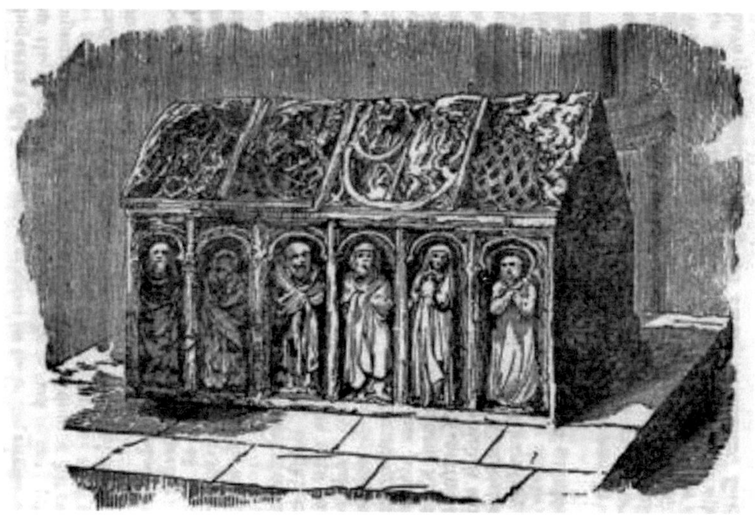

Ancient Monumental Stone in the Cathedral.

After the abbey of *Medeshamstede* was finished in 972, he ratified all the former charters which it possessed, and gave it the name of Burgh.

The first abbot of the monastery, after its destruction, was called Adulphus, formerly the king's chancellor; but having accidentally been the cause of the death of his only son, he could no longer live happily in the world, and he therefore endowed the abbey with all his wealth, and was elected its first abbot.

The monastery of *Burgh* was now in a more prosperous and wealthy condition than ever; all the neighbouring country was subject to it, and its possessions were so immense that its name was changed to *Gildenburg*. Adulphus, wishing to increase the value of the estates of the monastery and to encourage agriculture, had all

14

the surrounding forests cut down and the lands cultivated. He was afterwards made Archbishop of York, [992,] and the eloquent Kenulfus succeeded him in the reign of Ethelred. Kenulfus built a high wall round the monastery, part of which is still in existence. He was translated to the see of Winchester, in 1006, and was so celebrated for his virtue and learning, that he gave a character to the monastery, and the monks were for a long time afterwards considered the most enlightened and intelligent men in the island.

Elsinus was the next abbot of whom we read in connection with the monastery, and was remarkable for the number of relics which he had collected. Gunton tells us that the arm of St. Oswald[4] was the most famous, and Walter de Whittlesea informs us that King Stephen came to *Peterburgh* to witness the miracles which it is said to have performed. During the abbacy of Elsinus, England was invaded by the Danes under King Sweyn, in revenge of a massacre of his subjects by the order of King Ethelred. They landed in the north, and, having gained some advantages, proceeded southward to the fen country, which they plundered and laid waste with fire and sword. Heavy fines were extorted from the rich abbeys; that on Crowland amounting to £64,000 of the present value of money. Elsinus died in 1055.

Arwinus was then elected abbot, but he resigned in 1067 to Leofric. He was nephew to Earl Leofric, of Mercia, whose Countess, according to the chroniclers, redeemed Coventry from toll by riding naked through the streets of that town.

During the third year of this abbot, William the Conqueror invaded England, and we are told that Leofric fought for some time in the English army, but in consequence of ill health, was obliged "to return to his monastery, where he died on the third of the kalends of November, a.d. 1066." Braddo (or Brand) was the next successive abbot, but died after a rule of three years.

Thorold of Fescamp, who for some service rendered to the conqueror, had been appointed to an abbacy near Salisbury, was considered by William, on account of his soldier-like qualities, to be a fit person to transfer to the rebellious and disorderly neighbourhood of the Camp of Refuge, and he was accordingly appointed Abbot of Peterborough, in 1069.

Between the death of Braddo and the arrival of his successor, the second destruction of the monastery took place. A band of Danish soldiers, headed by Hereward de Wake, nephew of Braddo, attacked the monastery, and all the valuable treasures which it possessed were either taken away or destroyed. They then set fire to the building. The following is Gunton's account of the treasures which they captured; and, as it puts us in possession of much curious information concerning those times, we will give the extract entire:—"They took the golden crown from the head of the crucifix, the cross with the precious stones, and the footstool under; *duo aurea feretra* (two golden or gilded biers whereon they carried the saints' reliques, and other such like things, in procession), and nine silver ones; and twelve crosses, some of gold and some of silver. And, besides all this, they went up to the tower and took away the great table which the monks had hidden there, which was all of gold, and silver, and precious stones, and wont to be before the altar, with abundance of books, and other precious things, which were valuable, there being not the like in all England."

The monks were disconsolate at the loss of these valuable treasures, and the abbot solicited William the King to interfere for them, in order that they might be returned. It appears, however, that the conqueror did not pay much attention to their request; and it is probable that, as he had just after this depredation concluded a treaty of peace with the Danish sovereign, he was unwilling to do anything that should cause a breach of peace between them, especially as they were such troublesome and dangerous enemies. The greater part of the treasure was by some means once more restored to the monks,[5] and, according to the Saxon chronicler, they commenced from this time to build ramparts for their own protection, and for the security of the monastery. Tout Hill[6] in the vineyard field was raised at this time, and there is said to have been a subterraneous passage which ran thence to Croyland and Thorney. This hill was originally called Mount Thorold.

After the arrival of Thorold at Peterborough, being accompanied by 160 well-armed Frenchmen, he proceeded to turn his attention to the Camp of Refuge, situated near Ely; and, joining Ives of Taillebois in an assault upon it, was repulsed by Hereward de Wake, and taken prisoner, with many of the monks; nor was he liberated, according to Dean Patrick, until he had paid three thousand marks. After his liberation, he returned to the monastery, and made himself more odious to the monks than before. He was depraved and dissolute, and, to satisfy his licentious desires, he is said to have made free with the treasury. He introduced two monks likewise into the monastery, who were foreigners, and quite as unscrupulous as himself, in purloining the wealth of the abbey. He was afterwards made a bishop in France, but owing to his utter recklessness of conduct and morality, he was sent back to England four days after: was again admitted abbot of the monastery of *Peterburgh*, where he died in 1098, after an odious government of twenty-eight years.

During the reign of Henry I., the son of the Conqueror, Ernulphus became Abbot of *Peterburgh*. This event took place in the year 1107, and he made several important improvements in the monastery; built a new dormitory and refectory, and completed the chapterhouse, which had been left in an unfinished state for several years. He likewise enriched the convent by making an arrangement with all who held in rent the abbey lands to pay tithes to him, and, when they died, that they should give the third part of their estates to be buried in the church. Thus it was that the monastery continued to grow in wealth, and when Ernulphus was made Bishop of Rochester, which happened in 1114, the abbey was entitled to a tithe of 40,800 acres of land.

During the rule of his successor, John de Sais, the monastery was burned down. The fire is said to have occurred accidentally, and such was the violence of the flames, that they reached the village and consumed most of the cottagers' houses. The additions which Ernulphus had made to the abbey, however, are said to have escaped the general ruin.

CHAPTER II.

From the Foundation of the New Church, in 1117, to its dissolution as an Abbey by Henry the Eighth, in 1541; – embracing a period of 425 years.

In the first chapter of our history, we traced the rise and progress of the monastery of *Peterburgh* through a period of 462 years, at the expiration of which time we saw it burned to the ground, with all the treasures which it had accumulated. We have now to witness its restoration, and to follow it until we come to the nineteenth century, through all the ravages which it has survived.

At the time of the eventful destruction which we have mentioned [1116], John de Sais was abbot of the monastery, and had regained for it several of the lands which had been forfeited by his predecessors. He was, according to Gunton, a very learned man, and possessed great strength of mind and decision of character. He showed his energy by the prompt measures which he took to rebuild the abbey after its destruction, and to get all those lands, manors, and fees confirmed to it which it had so long enjoyed, and which continued daily to increase. It was a very long time, however, before the new monastery was built. John de Sais superintended it during his abbacy, but he lived only nine years after he had laid the foundation-stone (which ceremony he performed in the month of March, 1117), and the building was not completed at his death; nor did he succeed in securing to the monastery all its former possessions, although he exerted himself very assiduously to obtain them.

John de Sais was succeeded by Henri de Angeli, in 1128, of whom nothing of moment is recorded. He was a man of no character, and tried to injure the monastery in the estimation of the king, by speaking falsely of the brotherhood. Some writers say that he was detected in his villany by the king, who obliged him to resign his chair, and leave the country; others assert that he quitted England on account of other crimes. All historians agree, however, that he was a very bad man.

The appointment of the next abbot devolved upon the king, and Martin de Vecti was chosen by him to govern the monastery, in 1133. The monks received him with every expression of respect, as he was reported to be a man of profound erudition and good moral character. He began his rule by forwarding the erection of the new monastery, and it was during his abbacy that it was completed and re-dedicated—which latter ceremony was conducted with great pomp, and all the abbots of the neighbouring monasteries, with numbers of the barons and gentry, were present [1140]. It appears that De Vecti was very zealous in the work of improvement, and that he not only built a new gate to the monastery, but formed a new village on the western side of it; altered the place of wharfage, erected a new bridge, planted the present vineyard, and built many new houses near the abbey. He is also said to have re-built the parish church, then situate in St. John's close, in the precincts. The destruction of the castle, which stood near this church, is likewise attributed to this abbot. It is probable that it was situate upon Mount Thorold, or Tout Hill, as it is now called. This hill may yet be seen in a close on the north-western side of the cathedral.

De Vecti ruled twenty-two years, and died in 1155.

After the death of De Vecti, the monks resolved to maintain the right which they possessed of choosing their own abbot, and William de Waterville was elected by them to the government of the monastery: their choice was afterwards ratified by the king. Waterville was formerly a chaplain to Henry II., and having some influence with him, he regained for his abbey "the eight hundreds of that part of the country which had formerly been granted by the king's predecessors;" and, being firmly established in the monastery, he turned his attention to the improvement of the town. He founded a hospital for the sick in Spitalfield; built St. Martin's church and St. Michael's nunnery, at Stamford—besides settling a yearly sum upon the church of St. John Baptist,[7] *Peterburgh*—covering the monastery with lead, and founding the chapel of Thomas à Becket.

It is stated by Gunton, that this chapel is in "the middle of the arch of the church porch," but this is an error which it will be well to correct. The present school-house near the minster gateway is found to be the chancel of the chapel; and it is thus described by Kennel— "The chapel of the blessed Thomas the Martyr, near the outer gate of the abbey there."

After a government of 20 years, Waterville was deposed, at the instigation of the monks, by the Archbishop of Canterbury. No positive crime was alleged against him—at least the monks have not mentioned any in their accounts of the monastery.

The next abbot of whom we read is Benedict, a man of great learning, who was appointed to the rule of the monastery by the king in 1177, after he had held it in his possession two years. The abbot brought several relics to the monastery, and finished the chapel of Thomas à Becket. He was very zealous likewise in his endeavours to re-obtain the abbey lands which had been forfeited or seized during the rule of his predecessors; nor was he scrupulous of the means which he took to effect it: sometimes he took possession of them by force, and at others he tried to conciliate the usurpers by large sums of money and fair promises.

The monastery, during his government, underwent many important changes. He rebuilt the whole body of the church, "from the lantern to the porch;" and it is the opinion of Gunton, that the curiously painted ceiling which covers the middle of the building was of his workmanship. He likewise added several houses to those which were already within the precincts of the abbey, and built the present gate which leads to the west front of the cathedral, with a chapel over it, which was dedicated to St. Nicholas.[8]

Benedict likewise obtained a charter for holding a fair upon the feast of St. Peter, and a market to be held every Thursday. The fair was to continue eight days.

This abbot ruled seventeen years, and died in 1194.

Andreas succeeded Benedict, and rose gradually from a monk to a prior, and finally to an abbot. It is said that he was a good man, and secured the esteem of the monks by giving them the lands of Fletton and Alwalton to enrich their table. He ordered likewise six marks a year to be given out of the monastery funds to the infirmary. This donation was continued by his successors for a long time, but Abbot Walter, during his rule, directed that it should be employed in purchasing wine for the "pitanciary."

During the reign of Andreas there were several lands given to the "Eleemossynary," and the monastery was very flourishing. He governed seven years, and died in 1201. His body was entombed in the south aisle, with two of his brethren, under a Norman arch, beneath which is the following epitaph:—

Hos tres abbates quibus est prior abba Iohannes,

Alter Martinus, Andreas ultimus, unus

Hic claudit tumulus; pro clausis ergo rogemus.

Acharius succeeded Andreas in 1200. He was originally a prior of St. Albans, but was presented by King John to the abbacy of this monastery, on account of his many virtues and distinguished talents. He seems to have had the interest of the monastery at heart as greatly as any of his predecessors, and was engaged in several lawsuits with different landowners, in order to recover the lost possessions of the abbey. He gained the marsh of Singlesholt from the Abbot of Crowland "for a yearly acknowledgement of four stones of wax," and increased the number of his monks. He endowed the church with many valuable articles—such as silver basins for the great altar, with a case of gold and silver, set with precious stones, for the arm of St. Oswald! He gave likewise two large silver cups to the refectory, with silver feet richly gilt, according to Gunton, and four table knives with ivory hafts. He paid money off the monastery debts, and purchased houses in London, which he added to the abbey possessions.

During the festival of St. Peter, a large wax candle, of five pounds weight,[9] was set before the altar, and burnt day and night, until the festival was completed. This custom was observed in all other feasts of the saints in the abbey; and during the rule of Acharius the festivals were remarkable for their pomp and splendour.

This abbot ruled ten years, died in 1214, and was succeeded by Robert of Lindsay, or Lyndesheye.

It was during the rule of this abbot that one of the most interesting changes was effected in the monastery: the windows until this time had been "stuffed with straw," to keep out the cold and the rain; and, at an immense expense, he had thirty-nine of them adorned with glass, which enterprise gained for him a considerable amount of fame and esteem. Not content with this change in his own monastery, he extended his generosity to other parts, and built a chancel to the church at Oxney. He was confirmed by the king at Winchester, and received the benediction of the Bishop of Lincoln.

Being thus installed in his new office with so much honour, he directed his attention to the forest lands by which he was surrounded. By virtue of the forest laws, foresters let their cattle run at liberty to graze, and they frequently did much damage to the possessions of the monastery, and to the property of the town inhabitants. Lindsay therefore wrote to the king to try to "disafforest" the lands which were contiguous to the monastery, and he effected his object by payment of 1320 marks. Of his other improvements we read that "he made in the south cloister a lavatory of marble, for the monks to wash their hands in when they went to meals—their hall being near on the other side of the wall, the door leading into it being yet standing; the lavatory continued entire until the year 1651, and then, with the whole cloister, it was also pulled down."

About this time, in the reign of King John, England was the scene of those civil contentions which terminated in favour of the barons, and the attainment of a charter of liberties. A large number of the monasteries in England were, however, despoiled by the king before the fate of the war was decided, and amongst them was Crowland Abbey. It is likely that of *Peterburgh* escaped the fury of the king's soldiers, for we do not read of any outrage being committed upon it at that time in the monkish records. Lindsay wrote a history of the monastery, according to Pitseus, but he did not enrich the church library with any valuable additions. He ruled seven years, and died in 1222.

Alexander de Holderness was the successor of Lindsay, and was elected November 30, 1222. He was called Holderness from the place where he was born. This abbot made a number of improvements in his monastery, and enriched it with money and relics. He built, says Gunton, "*the solarium magnum* at the door of the abbot's chamber, and a *cellerarium* under it, and furnished the church also with that precious crystal vessel wherein the blood of Thomas à Becket was kept." He likewise built halls at Oundle, Castor, Eyebury, and other places. He was much beloved by the monks, and died, after a government of four years, in 1226.

An interesting incident in connexion with this abbot may here be mentioned. On the 2nd of April, 1830, when the workmen were making a foundation in the cathedral church for the erection of a new choir, they discovered beneath one of the slabs a stone coffin, which their curiosity led them to open. They were surprised to find that it contained the body of a man, with a large coarse garment around it, equipped with boots, and having a crosier by its side. There were several very remarkable things connected with this discovery. The boots were what are called "rights and lefts," and in a good state of preservation. The crosier was perfect, and a part of the body was hard, and of a copper-coloured hue, whilst the other part was decomposed. The body was headless, and a piece of lead was found lying in *place of the skull*, with this inscription upon it—

ABBAS: ALEXANDR:

These remains were gathered together, replaced in the shell, and buried in the south aisle, nearly opposite the burial place of Mary Queen of Scots.

Martin de Ramsey was chosen abbot after the death of Alexander. His election was sanctioned by the king, and he was confirmed by the Bishop of Lincoln, at Westminster. There is nothing remarkable recorded of this abbot. He "disafforested" several lands about *Peterburgh*, and added them to the possessions of the monastery.

During the rule of this abbot, Pope Gregory IX. ordered that when there should be an interdiction of the monastery lands, the monks should close their doors, and not allow the people to hear their prayers, or participate in them; but the privilege was granted to the monks of Peterborough to say the service in a low voice to themselves, the ringing of the bell being dispensed with.

Martin ruled six years, died in 1232, and was succeeded by Walter de St. Edmond, in 1233. It was during the government of this abbot that the monastery of *Peterburgh* was re-dedicated and consecrated with holy oil, by the Bishops of Lincoln and Exeter [1238], according to the decrees of the constitution of Otto.[10] The ceremony was attended with the usual pomp of such proceedings, and the possessions of the monastery were ratified anew. Walter de Whittlesea gives a very favourable account of the disposition of this abbot, and speaks very highly of his benevolence to King Henry, who was reduced to the necessity of seeking support from this and other monasteries. St. Edmond entertained the king twice at *Peterburgh*, in company with the queen and the young prince. He also "gave 60 marks towards the marriage of Margaret, his daughter, with Alexander III., King of Scotland," and increased the number of his monks to one hundred and ten. He made likewise three several journeys to Rome upon civil and ecclesiastical business. The cause of one of these journeys was this:—The Pope (Gregory, 1241) sent messages to *Burgh*, demanding that the abbot should give unto one of his favourites a certain yearly sum, or a number of lands equal to that sum, and the abbot refused to do so without the consent of the king who was patron of the monastery; and going to Rome to know the cause of such an arbitrary demand, he was reproved by the Pope in person, and treated with great indignity by the cardinals, and expelled the court. The abbot was so much grieved, by this cruel and ungenerous treatment that he never recovered, but died in the same year [1245], after having ruled twelve years with the greatest mildness, prudence, and benevolence. This story of the Pope's arbitrary conduct calls forth a very pithy couplet from Gunton—

"Rome gnaweth hands as dainty cates,

And when it cannot gnaw—it hates."

Walter was a learned man, and increased the books of the library. Gunton says "he was pious and merciful to all, exacted nothing unduly of his tenants, whether rich or poor; but if any poor man or woman made their necessities known to him, he would burst into tears, and take compassion upon them."

The next abbot of whom we read is William de Hotot, who was elected on the 6th of February, 1246. His rule was not favourable to the monastery. He lavished the possessions of the church upon his friends and kinsmen. His conduct was reprehended by the monks, and finally represented to the Bishop of Lincoln, when William, fearing he should be deposed, resigned his office, and retired upon an allowance from the monastery in 1249, after governing three years.

Mr. Owen Davys, in his Guide to the Cathedral, remarks that "it is a matter of great surprise that we have no record handed down to us of the exact date when that magnificent appendage to the Cathedral, the western front, was erected, though it must have been about this time. The name of the architect under whose directions this original and strikingly beautiful design was carried out is also buried in obscurity. This noble front is almost entirely built in the style usually known by the name of early English Gothic, of which it is, perhaps, the finest example we have now left us.

"It would seem that scarcely any time elapsed between the building of the western transepts of this monastic church and the commencement of the west front, as the style of the western transepts is Late Transition Norman, and in some places almost Early English, and that of the west front pure Early English. Now, as the Transition Norman gave place to the Early English in this country, about the commencement of the thirteenth century, it would seem probable that these western transepts were built at that time, probably during the government of Acharius [1200]; these works being carried on by Robert de Lindsay, his successor, might have been completed by him: the mixture of Early English work with that of the former style in them may thus be satisfactorily accounted for. It would seem, therefore, that these transepts were erected before the time of Walter St. Edmonds, and that the building of the west front probably followed immediately after the erection of them. Mr. Britton, in his 'History and Antiquities of Peterborough Cathedral,' page 56, refers the building of this interesting feature of the church to the times of Acharius and Robert de Lindsay. It would seem, however, that though it was probably begun in the time of the latter abbot, it was not finished till the time of John de Caleto, who came to the government of this abbey a.d. 1249. The reason for this opinion is the similarity of some of its details to those of the infirmary church, which was erected by this abbot. Some beautiful portions of this church are still to be seen. This abbot is said to have been a great builder; and it is probable that the refectory and south cloister were rebuilt by him; and that the door by which the Bishop usually enters the Cathedral, was inserted at the same time. The Chapel of St. Lawrance, which stood at the east end of the infirmary church, seems to have been erected about this time. There was an entrance into this chapel, from the infirmary church, through an arch, which is still standing, the chapel having been converted into a prebendal house."

Richard de London was elected abbot in 1274. He had held several offices in the monastery before his instalment, and being well acquainted with the discipline of the church, he governed well and wisely. He recovered the manor of Biggins, near Oundle, of the Earl of Clare, and his success was mainly owing to the eloquence of one of his monks, who pleaded the cause of the monastery in person, before the judge of assize at Northampton.

It was during the government of Richard de London that Prior Parys built and endowed the Lady Chapel.[11] This abbot ("when he was sacrist") also built one of the largest steeples of the church, and gave two bells to the monastery. He died in 1295, having ruled twenty years. In his reign the library and the monastery lands were increased considerably.

William de Woodford was next elected abbot. During the latter part of the rule of Richard, he had assisted him in performing the duties of abbot, which the latter was unable to do of himself, on account of his great age.

Swapham informs us that whilst William was abbot, the Pope taxed all the manors of the abbey.

Woodford is described as a fair and impartial man, of much kindness and benevolence, who added to the provisions of the monks,—obtained a charter for the possession of all the deer that might be slain on the monastery lands, and devoted his attention to the better regulation of the hospital of St. Leonard.[12] He died after a rule of four years, in 1299, and was succeeded by Godfrey de Croyland in the same year. This abbot, on his installation, was presented by Prince Edward with a silver cup, and had the confirmation fees returned to him by the Bishop's order.

The service in the chapel of Thomas à Becket was for a time suspended during this abbot's rule, in consequence of a violation of the sanctity of the place by certain officers, who, being in search of several men that had transgressed against the laws, and hearing they had taken shelter in the monastery, dragged them hence by force.

The Bishop of Lincoln therefore put his curse upon the place, nor was it without much persuasion that he granted an absolution.

The same year, being 1300, says Gunton, "a marriage being intended betwixt the heirs of Offord and Southorp, king Edward supposing himself to be interested therein, appointed inquisition to be made whether the disposal of that marriage belonged to him or the abbot of *Peterburgh*. And it being upon the inquisition certified that those heirs and their progenitors held their lands of the abbey of *Peterburgh*, the right of disposal of those heirs did therefore belong to the abbot, which the king, understanding, desisted." This right of disposal is well worthy of notice, as it illustrates the spirit of the time better than a great deal of writing.

Godfrey was remarkable for his generosity and sumptuous entertainments. The king and queen, with all their retinues, were provided for at the monastery, and once Prince Edward came with Peter Gaveston, and the abbot presented them with two magnificent robes.[13]

Godfrey added many beautiful improvements to his monastery, and built "the great gate-tower, over which was the chamber called the knights' chamber," being the gateway leading to the Bishop's Palace. The walls of this room were carved with knights and their coats of arms.

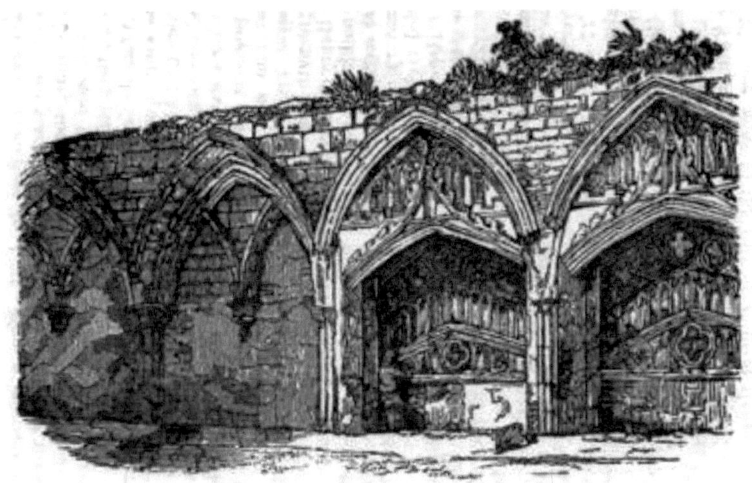

Peterborough Cathedral—Remains of Cloisters.

Whilst Edward was preparing for war against Scotland, he sent five successive times to this abbey for money to assist him in carrying on his enterprise, and Godfrey gave him in all about £500. His other gifts and entertainments were sumptuous and large, and the sum of money which he expended during his abbacy was £3646 4s. 3d. This remarkable man died in 1321, after a splendid rule of twenty-two years. The value of the monastery possessions in his time, about *Peterborough* alone, was £621 16s. 3d; but this sum was but a small portion of the vast property which then belonged to the church.

Adam de Boothby was the next abbot. He entertained the king, queen, and royal household, in the year 1327, which cost him £327 15s. Prince Edward, with his sisters and servants, were likewise hospitably treated at this abbey during a stay of eight weeks. Like Godfrey, Boothby was a generous man, but the expenses which the royal family cost him and his predecessors must have been a heavy impost upon the monastery. He died in 1338, in the eighteenth year of his rule.

Henry de Morcot was installed in February, 1338. There is nothing of any moment recorded of him, except that he was engaged in successful litigation with a baron for the recovery of some church lands. He died in 1346, having ruled eight years.

"Henry being dead, was buried betwixt the quire and the great altar, near unto his predecessor Adam. His grave being, in the year 1648, opened to receive the body of John Towers, late head bishop of this place, there was found a seal of lead (the instrument wholly consumed), having on one side these letters thus inscribed:—'Spa Spe,' over their several effigies; on the reverse—'Clemens P P VI.' (Gunton, p. 47-48). It is probable that the instrument was some indulgence gotten at the jubilee, which was but three years before."

Robert Ramsey succeeded to the abbacy in 1346, but of him nothing particular is recorded.

Henry de Overton was Abbot in 1361, and was followed by Nicholas, who was noted for his prudence and economy.

We now come to the rule of William Genge, who was elected in 1396, and ruled twelve years. He was, according to Gunton the first abbot of this monastery who was dignified with a mitre. In the supplement to Gunton's history, it is stated "that they put on mitres in token they had episcopal jurisdiction, and being advanced to the dignity of barons, and to sit in parliament which no other abbots had done." During his abbacy, the church which was then situate in St. John's close, in Boongate, was taken down, and re-erected on its present site. The cause of this removal was the fearful inundations to which, from its proximity to the fens, it was exposed.

Between 1408 and 1438 the monastery was presided over by John Deeping. During his abbacy great complaints were made of the conduct of the Monks, and the heads of the Benedictine order were summoned before the King at Westminster, to answer the charge of abuses, which they could not deny, but promised to reform.

Richard Ashton was appointed abbot in 1438, and ruled 33 years. He made many visits to the neighbouring monasteries, and likewise received many from their abbots. He granted several corrodies to persons who endowed his abbey. One to John Delaber, bishop of St. David's, is worthy of notice.—This John had his choice, whether to remain at *Peterburgh* for life, and receive a pension of £32 per annum, or retreat to the abbot's manor at Eyebury[14] with the same advantages.

There was another corrody granted to Alice Garton, the widow of Thomas Garton, who was a benefactor to the Cathedral, and whose name is engraved on stone, in characters of an hieroglyphic kind, over the large painted window at the west end of the building; it is well worth examining. It was in the year 1439 that king Henry granted a charter unto this abbot to hold a fair "for three days," commencing on St. Matthew's day, (O.S.) in a field, (now named the Mending,) which joins the counties of Huntingdon and Northampton together. This fair, on account of its vicinity to the bridge, was called "Brigge Fair," by which name it is still known. Ashton was called to parliament at Westminster, but being too infirm to attend, he deputed William Tresham, (probably one of his monks) to appear for him. He afterwards took the oaths of allegiance to his sovereign, at Coventry. During his rule it is stated that 33 monks died in the monastery, and many festivals were suspended in consequence, there not being a sufficient number left to perform the ceremonies. This abbot made several additions to the church; and the building at the east end, according to Britton, was commenced by him.

Mr. Davys is of opinion that, "though we read of no further additions being made to the church between the time of Godfrey, (1299), and that of abbot Ashton, much took place in this interval. Almost all the windows of the church must have been transformed from their original character into their present shapes, and those which escaped this mutilation, as in the transepts and clerestory, were filled with their present unsuitable tracery, about the conclusion of the fourteenth century.

"The porch, or chapel, now used as the Chapter Library, standing within the central arch of the West Front, was probably built soon after this time. The reason why it was erected will be evident to any one who will examine the front carefully; for it will be seen that the clustered column, between the northern and middle arch, leans out to a very great extent, and were it not for the support it receives from this chapel, very serious consequences must ensue. The whole front also leans to the westward, though not so much so as this column. This inclination is evidently of very early date, and probably took place shortly after the completion of the front. This chapel was therefore added as a support to the front; its insertion is, nevertheless, much to be regretted, as it materially diminishes the beauty of the finest part of the Cathedral.

"Many alterations, and additions, seems to have taken place in this abbey, during the time when the decorated style was prevalent in England; and consequently between the time when the Infirmary Church was built, and the last-mentioned structure was erected, at the west end of the church. Of these may be mentioned, the two elegant spires on the north and south towers of the West Front, and the great south-west tower of the church, which has since been materially diminished in height. The present Chapter School, which was originally the chancel of Thomas à Becket's Chapel, was also built at this period; its nave was taken down in the time of Abbot Genge, who presided here between the years 1396 and 1408, and the materials were given to the inhabitants of Peterborough to re-build their parish church with, in a more convenient situation. The eastern and western arches of the lantern must also have been altered into their present shape about this time, and the first story of a tower, which, if it had been completed, would have been one of the finest in England, built upon them: this is now remaining, and forms all the pretence that this Cathedral can show to a central tower."

Ashton resigned in 1471, to the Bishop of Lincoln, and was succeeded by William Ramsey, in the same year, who, with the assistance of prior Maldon, erected a "brazen eagle" in the church, to which the bible and mass book were chained. This eagle is now in the choir of the Cathedral, and used when reading the lessons. Ashton was indicted[15] in 1480, for releasing a felon from the gaol at *Peterburgh*, and accepting a bribe for the same. He was tried and convicted, and was obliged to find sureties for better conduct. The original judgment is yet retained in the chapter-house; with the names of the abbot's sureties. He died in 1496, after a rule of 25 years.

Robert Kirton was made abbot in 1496. During his rule the regulations of the monastery were in a measure broken up; many of the monks had become disorderly and even licentious, and one of them robbed the shrine of St. Oswald of a number of jewels, and other valuable articles, for the purpose of paying a woman in the town the wages of her prostitution. Others gave themselves up to bacchanalian riots in a neighbouring tavern, and, instead of devoting their nights to "prayer," gave themselves up to the vulgar "company of dancers and ballad singers."

These irregularities took place in the 19th year of this abbot's rule. They were, however, speedily terminated by the Bishop of Lincoln, who, hearing of such notorious infringements of the monastic rules, came in person to restore those licentious members of the fraternity to their duty.

Abbot Kirton had many contests with his tenants, "but notwithstanding," says Gunton, "he forgat not to enlarge and beautify his monastery, for he built that goodly building at the east end of the church, now commonly known by the name of the new building,"[16] wherein he placed three altars, opposite three pair of stairs, descending from the back of the great altar. He likewise built a chamber in the abbey house, which is still called "heaven-gate chamber." He made also a beautiful window in the great hall "overlooking the cloyster." He added many pictures to those which were already in the chapel of St. Mary, or the Lady's Chapel, as it is now called, all which have since been destroyed. The gate that leads to the deanery is likewise of his workmanship, and bears his signature in hieroglyphics, viz:—a Kirk, and a tun under it. This gate is a magnificent specimen of architecture, and should be seen by every person who visits Peterborough. Abbot Kirton ruled nearly 32 years, and died in 1528.

John Chambers was the last abbot, and was elected in 1528.

Cardinal Wolsey visited the abbey in the 17th year of the reign of Henry the Eighth, and washed and kissed the feet of fifty-nine poor people, which ceremony was called "keeping his maundy." He then gave them twelve pence, three ells of canvas, a pair of shoes, and divided a barrel of red herrings amongst them: he likewise sang mass himself on Easter-day, and absolved from their sins all those who heard him.

It was during the rule of Chambers that Queen Catherine, the first wife of Henry the 8th, died [July 1, 1535], and was buried in the monastery. Her tomb may be seen in the north side of the choir. The scaff which covered her pall was originally deposited at the back of the great altar. It was inwoven with silver, and was very massive and heavy.

CHAPTER III.

From the transformation of the monastery into a Cathedral during the rule of abbot Chambers, in 1541, to the present time.

The dissolution of the religious houses of England is one of the most important events recorded in our national history. It changed the whole aspect of civil and ecclesiastical affairs, and produced an entire revolution in the scheme of legislation.

John Chambers, who was the abbot of *Peterburgh* before these changes commenced, conformed to the new order of things, and was retained in office by the king, — the monastery being converted into a cathedral, and the abbot into a bishop. The new establishment consisted of a Bishop, a Dean, and six canons; besides these the statutes directed that there should be six Minor Canons chosen, among other good qualifications, for their skill in singing, by whom the services in the Cathedral, were to be conducted, according to the usage of the old Cathedrals. Of these, one was to be chosen as Precentor, to whom the other Minor Canons, the Organists, Lay Clerks, and Choristers, were to be subordinate. The chancel of Thomas à Becket's Chapel, already spoken of, was then converted into a school-room, in which the Choristers, and a certain number of other boys, were to receive a classical education at the hands of one of the Minor Canons appointed, for his superior learning, to the office of schoolmaster. Chambers governed 15 years in his new office. There is some dispute amongst the historians of this church about the time of his death, but it is generally agreed that the tablet to his memory is dated wrong, and that he died in 1556. There were two monuments erected to him, by his own orders, before his death; and this circumstance may account for the error in the date upon the tablets. One of the monuments was a beautifully executed statue of himself, in white chalk, but it was destroyed in 1643. The bishop adorned the doors of the church with carved images and hieroglyphics, one of which at the west front represents a sinner tormented by devils, though it is now much defaced.

From the death of Bishop Chambers to the accession of Richard Howland, in 1584, nothing of importance occurred. It was during his rule that the unhappy queen of Scots fell a victim to the vanity and jealousy of Elizabeth, in the castle of Fotheringhay.[17]

"Although that unfortunate Queen had been executed on the 8th of February, her body was not brought to Peterborough for burial till the night of the thirtieth of July following, when it was conveyed by torch-light from Fotheringhay Castle by Garter King at Arms, and other Heralds, with a guard of horsemen, in a chariot made for the purpose, covered with black cloth. The corpse was met at the entrance of the cathedral by the bishop, Richard Howland, and Fletcher, the dean of the cathedral, with others, who attended it in solemn procession to the vault appointed for it, in which it was immediately deposited. The vault was then covered, an opening merely being left through which the Heralds might deposit their broken staves. No service was said at the time, as it was agreed that it had better be done on the day fixed for the solemnization of the funeral. On the day following, there came to Peterborough all those persons of rank appointed to attend the funeral, for whom a grand supper was prepared at the bishop's palace. On Tuesday, the first of August, 1586, being the day fixed for the funeral, they all marched in order to the church, the Countess of Bedford being chief mourner. The funeral service was performed by the Dean of Peterborough; the prebendaries and choir of the Cathedral then sang an anthem, after which a sermon was preached by Wickham, Bishop of Lincoln. The officers having broken their staves and cast them into the vault, and the offerings appointed having been made to the Bishop and Dean and Chapter of Peterborough, the nobility and officers, who had attended the funeral, returned to the bishop's palace, where a sumptuous repast was provided, after which they all returned to their respective homes.

"The place where this queen was interred, is now marked by a marble slab directly under the doorway leading from the choir into its south aisle. Over this was erected a superb monument to her memory, which remained perfect until the time of the great rebellion.

"After the queen's body had lain at Peterborough about 25 years, her son, James I., wishing to have it removed to Westminster Abbey, wrote to the Dean and Chapter of Peterborough, requesting them to allow of the removal.[18] The corpse was accordingly taken from its grave at Peterborough, and removed to the place where it now lies, at Westminster, under the care of Richard Neile, Bishop of Coventry and Lichfield, on October 11th, 1612."

The next event of public interest happened during the bishopric of John Towers, in 1643; namely, the destruction and defacement of all the monuments and ornamental pictures of the cathedral, through the foolish prejudices and blinded bigotry of the puritanical followers of Cromwell, who destroyed every thing valuable within it, and spread terror over the surrounding country. The stately front, the curious altar-piece, and beautiful cloister, for which the cathedral was remarkable, were defaced and injured by them as they passed through the city, on their way to Croyland, which they were going to besiege, it having declared in favour of the king. To reduce that town, the Parliamentarian forces marched through Peterborough about the middle of the month of April. The first regiment that came did no harm to the church, for, being commanded by one Hubbart, who seems to have been a great improvement upon the puritanical leaders of that time, the soldiers received orders, in no way to injure the Cathedral. But unfortunately, about two days after, a regiment of horse arrived, commanded by Colonel Cromwell; and these men the morning after their arrival, commenced the work of destruction. They broke open the doors of the church, demolished the monuments, and turned the building into a stable.

The fury of Cromwell's soldiers is thus described in an old paper called: —

"A short and true narrative of the Rising and Defacing the Cathedral Church of Peterborough, in the year 1643."

"The next day after their arrival, early in the morning, they break open the church doors, pull down the organs, of which there were two pair. The greater pair which stood upon a high loft over the entrance into the quire, was thence thrown down upon the ground, and then stamped and trampled on, and broke in pieces.

"Then the souldiers entered the quire, and their first business was to tear in pieces all the common prayer books that could be found. The great bible indeed, that lay upon a brass eagle for reading the lessons, had the good hap to escape with the loss only of the apocrypha.

"Next they break down all the seats, stalls and wainscots that was behind them, being adorned with several historical passages out of the old testament, a latin distich being in each seat to declare the story. Whilst they were thus employed, they happened to find a great parchment book, behind the ceiling, with some twenty pieces of gold laid there, by a person a little before. — This encourages the souldiers in their work, and makes them the more eager in breaking down all the rest of the wainscot. The book was called 'Swapham,' and was afterwards redeemed by a person belonging to the minster for ten shillings.[19]

"There was also a great brass candlestick hanging in the middle of the quire, containing a dozen and a half of lights, with another bow candlestick about the brass eagle. These both were broke in pieces, and most of the brass carried away and sold.

"A well disposed person standing by and seeing the souldiers make such spoil speaks to an officer, desiring him to restrain them; who answered, *'See how these poor people are concerned to see their idols pulled down.'*

"When they had thus defaced and spoiled the quire, they made up next to the east end of the church, and there break and cut in pieces, and afterwards burn the rails that were about the communion table. The table itself was thrown down, the table cloth taken away, with two fair books in velvet covers; the one a bible, the other a common prayer book, with a silver basin gilt, and a pair of silver candlesticks beside. But upon request made to Colonel Hubbert, the books, bason, and all else, save the candlesticks, were restored again.

"Not long after, on the 13th day of July, 1643, Captain Barton and Captain Hope, two martial ministers of Nottingham or Darbyshire, coming to Peterburgh, break open the vestry, and take away a fair crimson satten table cloth, and several other things, that had escaped the former souldiers hands.

"Now behind the communion table there stood a curious piece of stone-work, admired much by strangers and travellers: a stately skreen it was, well wrought, painted and gilt, which rose up as high almost as the roof of the church, in a row of three lofty spires, with other lesser spires growing out of each of them. This now had no

imagery work upon it, or any thing else that might justly give of-
fence, and yet because it bore the name of the high altar,[20] was
pulled all down with ropes, lay'd low and level with the ground.

"Over this place, in the roof of the church, in a large oval yet to be
seen, was the picture of Our Saviour seated on a throne; one hand
erect, and holding a globe in the other, attended with the four evangelists, and saints on each side, with crowns in their hands, intended, I suppose, for a representation of Our Saviour's coming to
judgment. Some of the company espying this, cry out and say, 'Lo,
this is the God these people bow and cringe unto; this is the idol
they worship and adore.' Hereupon several souldiers charged their
muskets, (amongst whom one Daniel Wood, of Captain Roper's
company was the chief) and discharge them at it: and by the many
shots they made, at length do quite deface and spoil [the] picture.

"The odiousness of this act gave occasion (I suppose) to a common fame, very rife at that time, and whence *Mercurius Rusticus*
might have his relation, viz.: — that divine vengeance had signally
seized on some of the principal actors; that one was struck blind
upon the place; by a rebound of his bullet; that another dyed mad a
little after, neither of which I can certainly attest. For, though I have
made it my business to enquire of this, I could never find any other
judgment befal them then, but that of a mad blind zeal, wherewith
these persons were certainly possest.

"Then they rob and rifle the tombs, and violate the monuments of
the dead. And where should they first begin, but with those of the
two queens, who had been there interr'd: the one on the north side,
the other on the south side of the church, both near unto the altar.
First then they demolished Queen Katherin's tomb, Henry the
Eighth his repudiated wife: they break down the rails that enclosed
the place, and take away the black velvet pall which covered the
herse, — overthrow the herse itself, displaced the gravestone that lay
over her body, and have left nothing now remaining of that tomb,
but only a monument of their own shame and villany. The like they
had certainly done to the Queen of Scots, but that her herse and pall
were removed with her body to Westminster by King James the
First, when he came to the crown. But what did remain they served
in like manner; that is, her royal arms and escutcheons, which hung

upon a pillar, near the place where she had been interr'd [which] were most rudely pulled down, defaced and torn.

"In the north isle of the church there was a stately tomb in memory of Bishop Dove, who had been thirty years bishop of the place. He lay there in portraicture in his episcopal robes, on a large bed under a fair table of black marble, with a library of books about him. These men that were such enemies to the name and office of a bishop, and much more to his person, hack and hew the poor innocent statue in pieces, and soon destroy'd all the tomb. So that in a short space, all that fair and curious monument was buried in its own rubbish and ruines.

"The like they do to two other monuments standing in that isle; the one the tomb of Mr. Worm, the other of Dr. Angier, who had been prebendary of that church.

"In a place then called the new building, and since converted to a library, there was a fair monument, which Sir Humphrey Orm (to save his heir that charge and trouble), thought fit to erect in his own life time, where he and his lady, his son and wife and all their children, were lively represented in statues, under which were certain English verses written: —

> *"Mistake not, reader, I thee crave,*
>
> *This is an altar not a grave,*
>
> *Where fire raked up in ashes lyes,*
>
> *And hearts are made the sacrifice, &c.*

"Which two words, altar and sacrifice, 'tis said, did so provoke and kindle the zealots indignation, that they resolve to make the tomb itself a sacrifice: and with axes, poleaxes, and hammers, destroy and break down all that curious monument, save only two pilasters still remaining, which shew and testifie the elegancy of the rest of the work. Thus it hapned, that the good old knight who was a constant frequenter of Gods publick service, three times a day, outlived his own monument, and lived to see himself carried in effigie on a souldiers back, to the publick market-place, there to be sported withall, a crew of souldiers going before in procession, some with surplices, some with organ pipes, to make up the solemnity.

"When they had thus demolished the chief monuments, at length the very gravestones and marbles on the floor did not escape their sacrilegious hands. For where there was any thing on them of sculptures or inscriptions in brass, these they force and tear off. So that whereas there were many fair pieces of this kind before, as that of abbot William of Ramsey, whose large marble gravestone was plated over with brass, and several others the like, there is not any such now in all the church to be seen; though most of the inscriptions that were upon them are preserved in this book.

"One thing, indeed, I must needs clear the souldiers of, which *Mercurius Rusticus* upon misinformation charges them with, viz.:— That they took away the bell clappers and sold them, with the brass they plucked off from the tombs. The mistake was this: the neighbourhood being continually disturbed with the souldiers jangling and ringing the bells auker, as though there had been a scare-fire, (though there was no other, but what they themselves had made,) some of the inhabitants by night took away the clappers and hid them in the roof of the church, on purpose only to free their ears from that confused noise; which gave occasion to such as did not know it, to think the souldiers had stolen them away.

"Having thus done their work on the floor below, they are now at leasure to look up to the windows above, which would have entertained any persons else with great delight and satisfaction, but only such zealots as these, whose eyes were so dazzled, that they thought they saw popery in every picture and piece of painted glass.

"Now the windows of this church were very fair, and had much curiosity of workmanship in them, being adorned and beautified with several historical passages out of scripture, and ecclesiastical story; such were those in the body of the church, in the isles, in the new building, and elsewhere. But the cloister windows were most famed of all for their great art and pleasing variety. One side of the quadrangle containing the history of the Old Testament; another, that of the new; a third, a history from the first foundation of the Monastery of King Peada to the restoring of it by King Edgar; a fourth, all the kings of England downwards from the first Saxon king. All which notwithstanding were most shamefully broken and destroyed."

[But little remains to be seen of these famous cloisters beyond the mouldings of arches imposed in rough walls on each side. The five recesses in the south wall were partly the lavatories used by the Monks before entering the refectory by the richly cut door in the corner.]

"Every window had at the bottom the explanation of the history thus in verse:—

First Window.

Col. 1.

> "King Penda, a paynim, as writing seyth,
>
> "'Gate yese five children of Christen feyth."

Col. 2.

> "The noble Peada, by God's grace,
>
> "Was the first founder of this place."

Col. 3.

> "By Queen Ermenyld, had King Wulfere,
>
> "These twey sons that ye see here."

Col. 4.

> "Wulfade rideth, as he was wont,
>
> "Into the forest, the hart to hunt."

Second Window.

Col. 1.

"Fro' all his men Wulfade is gone,

"And 'suyth himself the hart alone."[21]

Col. 2.

"The hart brought Wulfade to a well,

"That was beside Seynt Chaddy's cell."

Col. 3.

"Wulfade askyd of Seynt Chad, —

"Where is the hart that me hath lad."

Col. 4.

"The hart that hither thee hath brought,

"Is sent by Christ, that thee hath bought."

Third Window.
Col. 1.

"Wulfade prayd Chad, that ghostly leech,

"The feyth of Christ him for to teach."

Col. 2.

"Seynt Chad teacheth Wulfade the feyth,

"And words of baptism over him he seyth."

Col. 3.

"Seynt Chad devoutly to mass him dight,

"And hoseled Wulfade Christy's knight."

Col. 4.

"Wulfade wished Seynt Chad, that day,
"For his brother Rufine to pray."

Fourth Window.

Col. 1.

"Wulfade told his brother Rufine
"That he was christned by Chaddy's doctrine."

Col. 2.

"Rufine to Wulfade said again, —
"Christned also would I be fain."

Col. 3.

"Wulfade, Rufine to Seynt Chad leadeth,
"And Chad with love of feyth him feedeth."

Col. 4.

"Rufine is christned, of Seynt Chaddys,
"And Wulfade, his brother, his godfather is."

Fifth Window.
Col. 1.

"Werbode, steward to King Wulfere,

"Told that his sons christned were."

Col. 2.

"Towards the chappel Wulfere 'gan goe,

"By guiding of Werbode, Christy's foe."

Col. 3.

"Into the chappel entred the King,

"And found his sons worshipping."

Col. 4.

"Wulfere in woodness his sword out drew,

"And both his sons anon he slew."[22]

Sixth Window.

Col. 1.

"King Wulfere, with Werbode yoo,

"Burying gave his sons two."

Col. 2.

"Werbode for vengeance his own flesh tare,

"The devil him strangled, and to hell bare."

Col. 3.

"Wulfere, for sorrow, anon was sick,

"In bed he lay, a dead man like."

Col. 4.

"Seynt Ermenyld, that blessed Queen,

"Counselled Wulfere to shrive him clean."

Seventh Window.

Col. 1.

"Wulfere contrite, hyed him to Chad,

"As Ermenyld him counselled had"[23]

Col. 2.

"Chad bade Wulfere, for his sin,

"Abbeys to build his realm within."

Col. 3.

"Wulfere in haste performed than,

"Brough that Peada his brother began."

Col. 4.

"Wulfere endued with high devotion,

"The abbey of Brough with great possession."

Eighth Window.

Col. 1.

"The third brother, King Ethelred,

"Confirmed both his brethren's deed."

Col. 2.

"Saxulf, that here first abbot was,

"For Ankery's, at Thorney, made a place."

Col. 3.

"After came Danes, and Brough brent,

"And slew the Monkys as they went."

Col. 4.

"Fourscore years and sixteen,

"Stood Brough destroyed by Danes teen."

Ninth Window.

Col. 1.

"Seynt Athelwold was bidden by God's lore,

"The abbey of Brough again to restore."

Col. 2.

"Seynt Athelwold to King Edgar went,

"And prayed him to help him in his intent."

Col. 3.

"Edgar bade Athelwold the work begin,

"And him to help he would not lyn."

Col. 4.

"Thus Edgar and Athelwold restored this place,

"God save it and keep it for his grace."[24]

"But to proceed, notwithstanding all the art and curiosity of workmanship these windows did afford, yet nothing of all this could oblige the reforming rabble, but they deface and break them all in pieces, in the church and in the cloyster, and left nothing un-demolisht, where either any picture or painted glass did appear; excepting only part of the great west window in the body of the church, which still remains entire, being too high for them, and out of their reach. Yea, to encourage them the more in this trade of breaking and battering windows down, Cromwell himself, (as 'twas reported,) espying a little crucifix in a window aloft, which none, perhaps, before had scarce observed, gets a ladder, and breaks it down zealously with his own hand.

"But before I conclude the narrative, I must not forget to tell, how they likwise broke open the chapterhouse, ransack'd the records, broke the seals, tore the writings in pieces, specially such as had great seals annexed unto them, which they took or mistook rather for the popes bulls. So that a grave and sober person coming into the room at the time, finds the floor all strewed and covered over with torn papers, parchments and broken seals; and being astonisht at this sight, does thus expostulate with them. Gentlemen, (says he,) what are ye doing? they answered, we are pulling and tearing the popes bulls in pieces. He replies, ye are much mistaken: for these writings are neither the popes bulls, nor any thing relating to him. But they are the evidences of several mens estates, and in destroying these, you will destroy and undo many. With these they were something perswaded, and prevailed upon by the same person, to permit him to carry away all that were left undefaced, by which means, the writings the church hath now came to be preserved.

"Such was the souldiers carriage and behaviour all the time during their stay at Peterburgh, which was a fortnights space: They went to church duly, but it was only to do mischief, to break and batter the windows and any carved work that was yet remaining, or to pull down crosses wheresoever they could find them; which the first founders did not set up with so much zeal, as these last confounders pulled them down.

"Thus, in a short time, a fair and goodly structure was quite stript of all its ornamental beauty, and made a ruthful spectacle, a very chaos of desolation and confusion, nothing scarce remaining but only bare walls, broken seats, and shatter'd windows on every side.

"And in the time of this publick confusion, two other things hapned not unworthy of relating: the one for the strangeness, the other for the sadness of the accident. The first was this, when now the church lay open to all comers, without locks and bars, and none to look after them, those specially that lead up to the leads above; two young children not above five years old, had got up the steeple by themselves, and having lost their way down, come to the place where the great bells hang. Here there was a large round space left purposely in the arch, when first built, for the drawing up bells or any other things, as there should be occasion. This place used to be safely closed before, but now it lay wide open, and was between thirty and forty yards off from the ground. The two children, coming hither and finding this passage, one, out of his childish simplicity, was for jumping down: No, (saies the other) let us rather swarm down, there being a bell rope then hanging down through that place to the clockhouse below. Now, this last they did, and a gentleman walking there beneath at that time, sees two children come with that swiftness down the rope, like arrows from a bow, who were both taken up for dead, on the place. This hapned on a Sunday ith' afternoon, in sermon time. The news coming into the parish church, that two children falling off from the minster were slain, the congregation were exceedingly disorder'd, so that the preacher could not go on for a time, every parent fearing it might be their own childrens case; till at length they understood the truth and certainty of all. For it pleased God by a strange and wonderful providence to preserve both these children, having no hurt but only their hands galled by the rope, and their feet a little stunted by the fall from the clock-house, where they were thrown off, the rope being fastened there, and this some four or five yards high. The persons, I suppose, are both living still; and one of them, (whose father was then one of the chief tradesmen of the town) since a grave minister, and rector of a parish in Northamptonshire.

"The other thing that hapned of more fatal consequences was this: — it being that time of the year when young lads are busie in rifling jackdaws nests to get their young, a scholar of the free-school, a son to a parliament officer, was got upon the top of the minster about this employment; who going along the cieling in the body of the church, and treading unwarily on some rotten boards, fell down from thence, upon the loft where the organ now stands, having his pockets filled with those inauspicious birds, and with the fall from so great a height, was slain outright and never stirred more.

"These two things hapned much about the same time, and in the time of that publick confusion and disorder. But to proceed in our intended narrative. These things I have related before were indeed the acts of private persons only, men of wild intemperate zeal, and who had no commission for what they did, but what was owing to the swords by their sides. Yet notwithstanding all these things seemed afterwards to be own'd and approved by the powers then in being, when they sold all the churches lands, and many fair buildings adjoyning to the minster, were likewise pulled down and sold by publick order and authority, such were the cloysters, the old chapter-house, the library, the bishops hall and chapel at the end of it: the hall was as fair a room as most in England; and another call'd the green chamber, not much inferior to it. These all were then pull'd down and destroyed; and the materials, lead, timber, and stone exposed to sale, for any that would buy them. But some of the bargains proved not very prosperous; the lead especially that came off the palace, was as fatal as the gold of Tholouse; for to my knowledge, the merchant that bought it, lost it all, and the ship which carried it, in her voyage to Holland.

"And thus the church continued ruined and desolate, and without all divine offices for a time; till at length by the favour of a great person in the neighbourhood, it was repaired and restored to some degrees of decency again; and out of the ashes of a late cathedral, grew up into a new parochial church, in which way it was employ'd and used ever after, untill the kings happy restauration. For Mr. Oliver St. John, chief justice then of the common pleas, being sent on an embassy into Holland by the powers that governed then, requested this boon of them at his return, that they would give him the ruin'd church or minster at Peterburgh; this they did accordingly, and he gave it to the town of Peterburgh for their use, to be employ'd as a parochial church, their own parish church being then very ruinous and gone to decay.

"Now the town considering the largeness of the building, and the greatness of the charge to repair it, which of themselves they were not able to defray, they all agree to pull down the ladies chapel as it was then called, an additional building to the north side of the minster, (being then ruinous and ready to fall) and to expose the materials thereof, lead, timber, and stone to sale, and to convert the mony that was made of them, towards the repairs of the great fabrick.

"All this they did, and appointed certain persons to oversee the work, and expended several summs thus in repairs, mending the leads, securing the roof, glazing several windows, and then fitting up the quire, and making it pretty decent for the congregation to meet in. And this they did, by taking the painted boards that came off from the roof of the ladies chapel, and placing them all along at the back of the quire, in such manner as they continue to this day.

"When the place was thus fitted up, and the devastations which the souldiers had made in some measure repaired, one Mr. Samuel Wilson, school master of the charter-house, in London, was sent down by the committee of plundred ministers, as they were then called, to be preacher, with a sallary of 160*l.* per an. in which employment he continued untill the kings return. Then Dr. Cofin, the antient dean of the church, after almost twenty years exile in France, return'd and re-assumed his right again, in the year 1660, about the end of July. He then after so long an interval renew'd the antient usage, and read divine service first himself, and caused it to be read every day afterward, according to the laudable use and custome, and settled the church and quire in that order wherein it now continues.

"But though the church was thus delivered from public robbers and spoilers, yet it was not safe from the injuries of private hands. For some ten or twelve years after, certain thieves in the dead of the night, broke into the church and stole away all the plate they could find, viz.: a fair silver bason gilt, and the virgers two silver rods, and a linnen table-cloth to wrap them in, which were never heard of to this day. This was the same bason that had been plunder'd by the souldiers, and recovered again, but irrecoverably lost now. Yet both these losses were soon repaired, one by Dr. Henshaw, bishop then of the place, who gave a fair new silver basin gilt; the other made up by Dr. Duport, then dean, who furnisht the virgers again with the ensigns of their office, by buying two new silver maces for the churches use.

"And thus is this history brought down at length within our own knowledge and remembrance; where we have seen what various fortunes this antient church has had, which now reckons at least one thousand years from its first foundation. It has been often ruinated, and as often re-edified. Once it was destroyed by Danes; twice consumed by fire; it escaped the general downfal of abbies, in Hen. the Eighth's time, though not without the loss of some of her fairest manners; and yet what that king took away in revenues, he added to it in dignity, by converting it from an abbey into a cathedral church. But the worst mischief that ever befel it, was that in the late rebellious times, when the church itself was miserably defaced and spoiled; and all the lands for the maintenance thereof, quite alienated and sold. And yet through Gods especial goodness and favour, we have lived to see the one repaired, the others restored, and the church itself recovering her antient beauty and lustre again. And that it may thus long continue, flourish and prosper, and be a nursery for vertue, a seminary for true religion and piety, a constant preserver of Gods publick worship and service, and free from all sacrilegious hands, is the earnest and hearty prayer wherewith I shall conclude this discourse."

CHAPTER IV.

Historical account of the building of the monastery, and description of the architectural peculiarities of the present cathedral.

Having in the preceding chapters given a brief history of the former monastery and present cathedral of Peterborough, up to the present time, it now remains for us to say something of its architectural peculiarities, and to notice some of the remarkable relicts of antiquity which are still to be found within its walls. It has already been stated, that in the year 655, the foundation for a monastic institution was laid at *Medeshamstede*; that it was completed seven years afterwards;—and was destroyed by fire in 870. The architectural character of the building at this period cannot be strictly ascertained; but, from the accounts given of it by monkish writers, it is supposed to have been of the pure Saxon style. The monastery was again re-built in 966, and again destroyed by the lawless hands of barbarian invaders. Five successive times did it undergo various changes of ruin and desolation, until the year 1117, when a new building was raised upon the foundations of the old one, and many additions were made to it;—extending its circuit, and improving its architectural appearance.

The immense stones which were laid as the foundation of the minster of *Medeshamstede*, is a sufficient proof of the vastness and massive strength of the building which was raised upon it;[25] — yet, as we have no definite information respecting the size of the monastery, we must leave it to be imagined by the reader, and proceed with the "new church," which was commenced in 1117, under the rule of John de Sais, and which we have already noticed in the first chapter of our history.

This John was a Norman by birth, and an admirer of the Norman style of architecture, which is discernable throughout the whole of this great building. That there is a mixture of style, however, in the monastery, is admitted on all hands;—nor could it well have been otherwise, if we take into consideration the different character of the ages in which additions were made to it. Still the leading features of the building clearly show that they are of Norman origin; and in this opinion we are supported by Mr. Britton, who says, "I cannot consent to discontinue this phrase, [viz. that the cathedral is a specimen of Norman architecture,] although it offends certain critics, who manifest more prejudice than discrimination in their reprobatory animadversion. That the Normans not only employed a peculiar style and character in the buildings of their own provence, and in England, after they possessed this country, is sufficiently proved by history, by the older edifices still remaining, and by the admission of the best informed antiquaries. It seems to me therefore absurd, as well as false, to say there is no Norman architecture—that the term is misapplied,—that the Normans were incompetent either to invent a novelty in art, or improve upon any thing of their Saxon predecessors. The instance of the building before us, which is said by its monastic historians to have been raised between the years 1117 and 1250, is sufficient evidence to confute the reasoning, or rather dogmatic assertions, of those who wish to exalt the Saxons by depreciating the Normans: and we have a still stronger confutation of this theory in the style and general character of the Trinity chapel, Canterbury, the history of which is well authenticated and generally credited. That it is a novelty and great beauty in architecture can only be disputed by those who are blinded by prejudice, or influenced by obstinacy and bad taste."[26]

During the prelacy of Bishop Marsh, 1819-1839, great efforts were made to restore the cathedral to its original beauty, under the auspices of Dr. Monk, then Dean of Peterborough, and afterwards Bishop of Gloucester. "By him the noble west front, which he found in a very ruinous state, was perfectly restored from top to bottom; six-and-thirty windows were opened in various parts of the church, which were built up, and two Norman doors were brought to light, which had been hidden under mean depressed arches."

It may, perhaps, be desirable to describe the different portions of the building in the order in which they present themselves to the visitor, and in doing this, we shall avail ourselves of the excellent remarks made by the Rev. Owen Davys, son of bishop Davys, in his work on the cathedral, and also of the superior talent of a gentleman, formerly well known in this city, (the Rev. T. Garbett,) who has investigated, with great care, the whole plan of the building, and has laid the result of his researches before the public.

Western Gateway.

First, then, is the ancient western gateway, built by Benedict, and though it has since been much altered, a considerable part of the original structure remains: "The western side has been faced with Perpendicular work, and an arch of that character has been built in front of the original Norman arch, above which is a very elegant arcade, the alternate arches of which have small windows within them; these light the chamber over the gateway which occupies the situation of the chapel of St. Nicholas. The lower roof of this gateway is a good specimen of a plain Norman roof, being groined with bold cross ribs. The arcades on the right and left hand, which have lately been very judiciously restored, are also worthy of notice; one of the arches in each arcade is considerably larger than the others, and forms a door-way. Above the arch, on the east side of this gateway, is a window which may strike the architect at first sight as being somewhat peculiar. It is in reality a part of an ancient Perpendicular shrine, which formerly existed in the cathedral, of which a portion is still standing in the northern part of the new building; it was brought there, and turned to its present use as a window, some time ago."

Thomas à Becket's Chapel.

On the left hand, as we pass through the gate, is the grammar school-room, formerly the chapel of Thomas à Becket, who was assassinated at Canterbury, and canonized by the catholics as a saint and a martyr. "The chancel of this building is of a very Late Decorated character, in fact so late as almost to come under the denomination of Transition from that style to Perpendicular; it has, on the south side, two windows, each of three lights, which appear, at first sight, to be Decorated, but, upon further examination, the architectural student will perceive, by a tendency to right lines in the tracery, that they are of Transition character, of which they form good examples. The east window of this chancel is a very good one, it is of five lights, and the tracery is very beautiful, though of a description not at all uncommon; in fact most of the Decorated windows in parish churches throughout Northamptonshire, which have any pretensions to size or beauty, have their tracery of this form, as, for instance, the east window of Higham Ferrers church, and many others. Above this window is an elegant pierced cross, probably of the same date as the window itself. The parapet of this chancel has nothing worthy of notice about it; it is like the rest of the building, of plain Late Decorated character."

Palace Gateway.

On the right of us, is the magnificent gateway which leads to the bishop's palace, over which is a chamber, called the knights' chamber. "This gateway is of somewhat peculiar Early English character, having a fine groined roof, springing from very beautiful clustered shafts. A line of arches, each of which contain within them two smaller arches, continues along either side of the interior; which is entered on the north and south sides, through fine and lofty arches supported by clustered columns. The bases of all these columns, like those of many others about the remains of this abbey, are covered with soil which the lapse of years has caused to accumulate around them; this of course much diminishes the height of each shaft. This beautiful gateway is flanked at its angles by square turrets, each ornamented, as also is the apex of the gable, with a fine niche, which has within it a figure of an unusually large size. The niches on the south side, contain the figures of St. Peter, St. Paul, and St. Andrew; those on the north, contain the representations of King Edward II., Abbot Godfrey de Croyland, and the Prior of the Abbey of that time, in full Benedictine costume.

West Front.

"The splendid front of the building is the most interesting and important of its members. This beautiful and original composition cannot fail to strike the mind of the beholder with awe and admiration; the first sight of it usually makes an impression on the memory which is not easily obliterated. It is indeed one of the finest specimens which the universe can produce, of the Pointed style of architecture. As a west front, scarcely any in this kingdom can be brought into comparison with it for beauty of proportion, and elegance of design. The west fronts of the cathedrals of Wells, York, and Lichfield have been mentioned as surpassing it in some respects; and in point of richness of detail, the two first may be perhaps considered as superior to it; but they all of them fall far short of Peterborough in the grandeur of their general effect.

"The outline of this front forms a regular square of 156 feet, that being the height of the side spires, and also the extreme width of the building. Its plan consists of three lofty arches of the same height, of which that in the middle is considerably the narrowest, the two side ones being of equal dimensions. These rest on triangular piers faced with shafts. At either extremity of this arcade are two lofty turrets, flanked at the angles by clustered columns, instead of buttresses, which run the whole height of the turrets. These turrets connect the arcade with the western wall of the church, from which it is distant fifteen feet, which gives the appearance of great depth and beauty to the arches." [*Davys' Guide.*]

"There was, perhaps little or no interval between the completion of the nave in the Circular style of architecture, and the erection of the north-west tower, in the Lancet, or first style of the Pointed. The original plan of the front, like that of Lincoln, comprised, no doubt, two towers rising at the western extremity of the side aisles of the nave, having a Norman base with circular lights, and an additional transept, projecting north and south beyond the line of the side aisles. But before this design could be carried into execution, architecture itself had undergone a change; pointed arches were substituted for circular ones, and slender isolated columns for the clustered shaft, or solid cylinder. Hence the difference in style of the tower just referred to: the string moulding at the base of it, together with the superstructure, and the pinnacles and pediment which surmount the adjacent transept, being all of a later order than the work of the nave: and hence also the union of both styles in the transept itself — its lofty arches, parallel to the side walls, being highly pointed, but with the zigzag ornament, and resting on Norman shafts; and the doorways of the front having circular heads, in accommodation to the arches of the nave, but with pointed mouldings and pillars.

"The tower, towards the south, appears never to have been finished, although unquestionably included in the architect's design. The present base, above the transept, is of a comparatively modern date, and altogether inferior to the work of the north-west tower. In the progress of great undertakings it not unfrequently happens that fresh objects present themselves to the mind, which at first were not thought of. Such appears to have been the case in respect of this cathedral, the architect of which, while completing the front, seems to have caught a new idea — that of erecting two lofty turrets beyond the outer angles of the transept, towards the west, and of converting the intermediate space into a sort of piazza, by arches constructed in front of the nave and closed in above by a vaulted roof. This idea so unique and at the same time so splendid, he was enabled to realize: and posterity, at the distance of six centuries, beholds with ineffable delight and admiration, a composition, the outlines and details of which, for their beauty and variety, render it one of the noblest facades in existence. Towards the north and south are two lofty turrets, flanked at the angles by clustered shafts, rising from a projecting base and crowned with spires, the height of which from the ground, makes a square with the breadth of the front. The space between these turrets is occupied by three pointed arches, reaching the whole height of the upper walls of the nave, and resting on triangular piers, which are faced with clustered shafts like those of the turrets, and terminate in octangular pinnacles, resting each upon a square basement, and divided by a moulding into two stages, the upper one of which is perforated with narrow lights, edged with the dog-toothed quatrefoil. The sides of the pier are lined with isolated columns in channelled recesses, each column sustaining a ribbed moulding of the arch above, and the whole series being finished with interlaced and foliated capitals.

"The centre arch is narrower than the outer ones, the reason of which will appear when we look at the situation of the doorways opening into the side aisles of the nave. Had the architect designed the three arches of equal breadth, the piers which sustain the centre arch must have stood immediately in front of these door-ways, or the outer arches must have been so contracted as to bring the turrets within the line of the transept, and thereby conceal, in part at least, the towers behind.

"This circumstance of itself shows that the turrets, piers, and arches, as they now exist, formed no part of the original plan. The interstices between the pillars which sustain the centre arch differ from those of the outer arches, in that they are chequered at regular distances with clumps of foliage, as if exuberance of ornament were designed to compensate for inequality in other respects. This inequality has been still further obviated by the erection of a porch, which, after a minute inspection, appears to have been inserted by way of support to the central piers, both of which had previously swerved from the perpendicular, as may still be seen. Over each arch rises a lofty pediment, bounded by the wave and billet ornaments, and surmounted by a perforated cross. The spandrils formed by the base of the pediment and the arches beneath, severally contain, first, a deeply recessed quatrefoil, above this two trefoil arches, and still higher two pointed arches, resting on slender pillars, and filled with statues,—and also a hexagon, the featherings of which clasp a human head.

"The pediments contain each a large circular light, with other apertures and niches. The circle of the central pediment is divided by mullions into eight lights, under trefoil arches radiating from an orb. Those on the sides are divided into six lights, the featherings of which are very beautiful. The mullions, or radii, are all faced with small pillars and capitals, and lined with the dog-toothed quatrefoil. The outer moulding of the central circle is composed of closely compacted trefoils, that of the others has the wave ornament. At the base of each circle is a series of trefoil arches, rested on isolated columns, four of which admit light into an apartment above the vaulting, and three contain statues. The intermediate spaces formed by the circle and the pediment, contain two niches, one on each side and another above, all filled with statues. The niche in the apex of the central pediment contains a statue, apparently of St. Peter, to whom the church is dedicated, representing the apostle with the mitre, pall, keys, and other insignia of the bishop of Rome.

"The turrets, before mentioned, are divided by the round moulding and string courses into six stages, which are empannelled in front with arches of different forms and dimensions. In the first stage from the ground, and rising from a channelled base, are two lofty pointed arches resting on slender pillars. In the second stage are four trefoil arches similarly supported; this range is continued round the facings of the inner wall immediately over the doorways, and forms the base of the windows. The third stage contains one pointed arch, intersected by a pillar in the centre, with curved mouldings, forming two lesser arches; which last are again subdivided by pillars sustaining one circular arch in the centre, and segments of arches on the sides.

"The interstices above contain two trefoil arches, with brackets at the base for the figures. The mouldings of the outer arch, with the sides of the pillars and all the sub-divisions, are studded with the dog-toothed quatrefoil. In the fourth stage, are two deeply recessed pointed arches, resting on clustered pillars; immediately over these is a string course of stemmated trefoils, which is continued round the front, the transepts, and the base of the north-west tower, together with the more modern base towards the south. In the fifth stage are four trefoil arches, like those of the second stage: these lie parallel with those at the base of the pediments, already described, and with those also of the side transepts. The sixth stage contains four long and narrow pointed arches, having corbels in the space above, and resting, like the whole series of arches below, on slender isolated columns, with prominent foliated capitals: above these is a string course of rosettes, forming the base of the parapet. Thus far the two turrets are strictly uniform; but in the parapets, by which they are surmounted, and in the pinnacles, which terminate the clustered shafts, there is a marked difference.

"The parapet of the north turret consists of the wave ornament, with double featherings and intersections: the pinnacles at the angles are hexagonal, corbelled at the base of the pyramid with human heads, and finished above with crockets and finials.

"The parapet of the south turret contains a series of quatrefoils, while the pinnacles at the angles are beautifully blended with the clustered shafts, so as to form a regular and continuous course and termination; the mouldings are carried up in high pointed pediments, and from these a cinquefoil arch at each angle, surmounted also by a pediment, with a quatrefoil in the spandril, connects them with the spire in the centre, and sustains a lofty triangular pinnacle, which, like the pediments below, is decorated with crockets and a finial. In this respect the south spire differs from the other, which has no connection with the side pinnacles. Both are pierced with pointed windows in two ranges, four in each range, divided by mullions, and crowned with crocketted pediments; and the apex of each is terminated by a finial and a cross, included in the extensive repairs carried on by the present dean[27] and chapter.

"The style of these spires, with the parapets and pinnacles, marks them out as a later work than the turrets beneath; and we may infer from the similarity of their details to those of the porch, that they formed a part of the repairs and alterations which the whole front appears to have undergone when the appendage was inserted; and when the central window of the nave was enlarged, and that, and the others which now enliven the inner wall, were filled with perpendicular tracery. The porch is vaulted with stone, and is entered by an obtuse arch, over which is an elliptical window, divided by mullions into six lights under cinquefoil arches, which are again subdivided in the head into lesser arches.

"The spandrils formed by the curve of the arch, and the base of the window, are enriched with circles, clasping shields of arms, and rosettes with other devices. The arches and windows are bounded by buttresses, which are broken by offsets and empannelled with niches. Besides these, the porch is flanked with staircases, one on each side, forming three parts of an octagon, and leading to an apartment now used as a library. The summit is closed with an embattled parapet, having a pediment at each end, and one in the centre. The surface of the walls is enriched with canopied niches, pilasters, brackets, panel work, and string courses in all the wildness and profusion which distinguish the last stage of gothic architecture.

"Besides the arch before mentioned, the porch has two smaller arches, north and south, parallel with the piazza formed by the great arches and piers of the front, and keeping up the communication with its opposite extremities. Over these also are mullioned windows with blank interstices.

"The great window of the nave, the outer arch of which is obviously an alteration from the original design, is divided by mullions into five lights, — those of the side aisles into three lights, both under cinquefoil arches, and the lancet windows of the transepts into two lights, under trefoil arches: these windows are parted, each by an embattled transome into an upper and lower range of lights, and the heads filled with subordinate tracery.

"The door-ways beneath are exceedingly rich, and in point of execution and delicacy of detail perhaps the finest portions of the front.

The central door-way is divided by a pillar, rising from a carved cylindrical base into two smaller arches; but the whole design and finish cannot be made out, in consequence of the introduction of the porch, the foundation and butments of which are built against it.

"The arches of the side door-ways are lined with isolated columns, receding in the manner of perspective; the ribbed mouldings between these columns, the interlaced and pendent foliage of the capitals, and the multiplied mouldings of which the arches above are composed, cannot be too closely examined, or too much admired. This is that peculiar style of gothic architecture, in which the beauty of the pointed arch, with its accompaniments is best discerned; and, therefore, it is that judges are wont to give it the preference over all subsequent alterations and refinements. The spaces between these door-ways, like those of the windows over them, are empannelled with pointed arches, subdivided by smaller arches, and resting on slender pillars.

"From the description thus given of this stately front, the reader will perceive that it was begun in one age, and finished, as we now behold it, in another. Some discrepancies of style may therefore be expected to present themselves, but these are so eclipsed by the grandeur in its leading features, that the eye takes in the whole as a single conception, and overlooks, in its contemplation of such a magnificent association of objects, the marks of difference that exist between the efforts of earlier and later genius."[28] —The Purbeck pillar, which divides the greater arch of the West door into two lesser arches, has a curiously sculptured base, apparently representing a sinner being tormented by devils.

Gateway and Deanery.

As we cross the square to the north-eastern side of the church, we pass another gateway, which leads into the deanery, which is a fine specimen of architecture, and bears the monogram of its builder, viz.—the letter R, a kirk, and a tun, [R. Kirkton] and we then enter at once into the

Burial Ground.

Exterior north, east, and south.

60

A finer association of beautiful and mournful objects could not well be imagined than is here presented to us. The most graceful trees, arranged in delightful groups, hang over the decayed tombs, which are carpeted to their base by a green sward, covered with flowers. As we pass along, we get a view of the deanery, and at the end of the eastern part of the church we see Tout Hill with the Training College for schoolmasters on the left, and the pretty villa in the vineyard, with a splendid avenue of old elm trees leading to it by a broad gravel walk. We pass likewise the large painted window, and as we turn the eastern end of the building, we catch a glimpse of the ruins of the infirmary and great hall, with their magnificent arches and ivy clad columns. Proceeding round to the southern side of the cathedral, we enter the square, where are the ruins of the cloisters, through a fine old door-way with a pointed arch, surmounting others of a circular form, and enriched with sculptural mouldings and figures. The southern and western walls of the cloisters remain, and contain a singular variety of tracery, mouldings, columns, and door-ways. Two door-ways to the southern aisles of the nave are also seen in the cloisters—one having a semicircular arch, with archivolt mouldings, enriched with the chevron and other Norman ornaments; the other in the pointed or gothic style, with raised mouldings, and supported by slender shafts at the sides.[29] At the southern extremity of the cloisters is another door-way of the same style and character as that by which we entered them, which leads through the bishop's garden to the palace.[30] Passing along the western wall of the cloisters we go through a plain Norman door-way, which brings us again, by a narrow passage, to the west front of the cathedral.

The Dimensions

Of the several parts of the Cathedral are as follows: —

The breadth of the west front, measuring from corner to corner on the outside of it, is 156 feet.

The length of the whole cathedral, measured on the outside of it, is 471 feet. In this measurement are included the most prominent buttresses at the west and east ends.

The distance from the inside of the west door of the cathedral to the organ screen at the entrance into the choir is 267 feet.

From the organ screen to the altar screen, 117 feet.

From the altar table to the east window 38 feet. So that the distance from the west door to the east window is 422 feet.

The length of the two cross aisles or transepts within, including the diameter of the lantern, 180 feet.

The breadth of the nave within, measuring from the south wall to the north wall, is 78 feet; that is half the breadth of the west front.

From the floor of the nave to its painted wooden roof is a height of 81 feet.

The height of the lantern within the church is 135 feet. The whole height of it without is 150 feet.

The height of each gothic arch at the west front of the cathedral is 82 feet.

The distance from the ground to the top of each pinnacle at the corners of the west front is 156 feet; that is, the same with the breadth of the front.

The Interior of the Building

is grand beyond conception. The northern and southern aisles are formed by massive ranges of pillars, supporting vast arches of singular simplicity and beauty. The great pictured roof or ceiling in the nave of the church, is a curious specimen of fanciful ingenuity. The divisions are of a diagonal form filled with various devices, some representing kings and queens or early patrons and founders of the monastery: others being of an hieroglyphical character.

"The nave and its aisles," says Mr. Britton, [page 70] "display a uniform style of architecture in their arches, piers, triforia, and walls; but the windows of the clerestory, triforia, and aisles are all of a later date, and are evident insertions in the original walls,— excepting indeed the exterior walls of the triforium, which appear to have been raised, and a new roof formed when some great alterations were made to the church. On the eastern side of the transept is an aisle, the southern division of which is separated into three chapels, or oratories, as they were originally appropriated, but now used as appendages to the choir. Over this aisle is a triforium, behind an arched screen, which extends along the aisles of the choir to their junction with the new work."

The lantern is another remarkable feature in this building. It "is open to the vaulted roof," and is a fearful height to contemplate.

The choir is nearly of the same kind of architecture as the transept. Its vaulted roof is boarded, but assumes an imitation of the florid pointed style,—being disposed in several compartments by thin ribs. Over the altar end it is painted with an emblematical representation of Christ as a vine, and his disciples the branches. The remaining portion of the roof, which had been painted white and yellow, has also been recently restored to its original character, the bosses being gilt and the spandrils painted bright blue and richly ornamented.

Until the year 1827, the choir of this cathedral was composed of deal painted to resemble oak, and "although in good repair," was generally allowed to be "unworthy of the magnificent structure to which it belonged." At the suggestion, and under the immediate patronage of the then dean and chapter, a subscription was entered into for the purpose of erecting a new choir and organ screen; and the sum of £5021 11s. 0d. was shortly obtained towards that object. The architect employed was the celebrated Mr. Blore, who, assisted by Mr. Ruddle, of Peterborough, completed the work in 1830.

The organ screen is composed of clunch stone, and is decorated with spiral turrets, having a number of gaudily painted shields in the spandrils, which, together with the rainbow hues of the organ pipes, give it an appearance rather offensive to modern taste, although strictly in accordance with the rest of the work, which is in the style of the 1st and 3rd Edward.

On the right of the entrance to the choir is a brass plate with the following inscription:—

this
ORGAN SCREEN
with the

CHOIR AND ALTAR SCREEN,
was erected a.d. mdcccxxx.
by subscription
from the members of this cathedral church,
the inhabitants of the
city and neighbourhood of peterborough,
and
other admirers of ecclesiastical architecture,
under the auspices of
THE VERY REV. JAMES HENRY MONK, D.D.,
dean.

The New Pulpit,

erected to the memory of the Rev. John James, D.D., for 40 years Canon of the Cathedral, has a most massive appearance. The principal material used in its construction is Dumfries stone, with pillars of Devonshire and Greek marble. The body rests on a centre marble base, with corner pillars of Greek marble. At each corner of the pulpit stand figures of the four evangelists. The three panels are richly carved, and in the centres are cut the figure of a lamb, a Norman cross, and the letters I.H.S. Greek marble has been employed as pillars for the stair rails, along which and around the upper part of the pulpit is Devonshire marble. The following inscription inlaid with gold is cut in the Greek marble bordering:—"In Memoriam. Johannes James, S.T.P., hujus Ecclesiæ Cathedralis XL.; Anno Canonici P.C. Filii Superstites A.D. mdccclxxiii, O.B. xv Dec. mdccclxviii." The arms of the See and the Dean and Chapter are cut in the stone body. The architect was Mr. Barry, of London, and the work was executed by Messrs. Field, Poole, and Sons, Westminster.

Monuments.

There are very few ancient monuments remaining in this cathedral, the greater portion having been destroyed by Cromwell's soldiers. A brazen eagle, or lectern, in the centre aisle of the choir, from which the daily lessons are read; an ancient stone at the east end of the building, till lately supposed to be commemorative of the murder of eighty-four monks by the Danes, in 870;[31] and a picture of old Scarlet, who died in 1594, aged 98, are the principal objects of interest.

Turning to the left, as you enter the west door of the cathedral, hangs the portrait of this celebrated character, who buried within the walls of the cathedral, Catherine of Arragon, who died at Kimbolton Castle, in 1536; and Mary Queen of Scots, who was executed at Fotheringhay Castle fifty-one years afterwards. The accompanying engraving is a representation of the old sexton, with his spade, pickaxe, and other emblems of office.

In the south-west or opposite corner of the nave, is an *ancient font*, originally composed of native marble, obtained from the quarries at Alwalton.[32] The basin of this font was, for many years, in one of the prebendal gardens, where it was placed upon the base of an old Norman pillar, and used for holding flowers, but was removed by Dr. Monk, when dean of Peterborough, to the chapterhouse. The celebrated statuary, Mr. Gresley, of Oxford, put it upon its present pediments, which are composed of Purbeck marble, and it was then placed where it now stands. It is considered a very fine piece of workmanship.

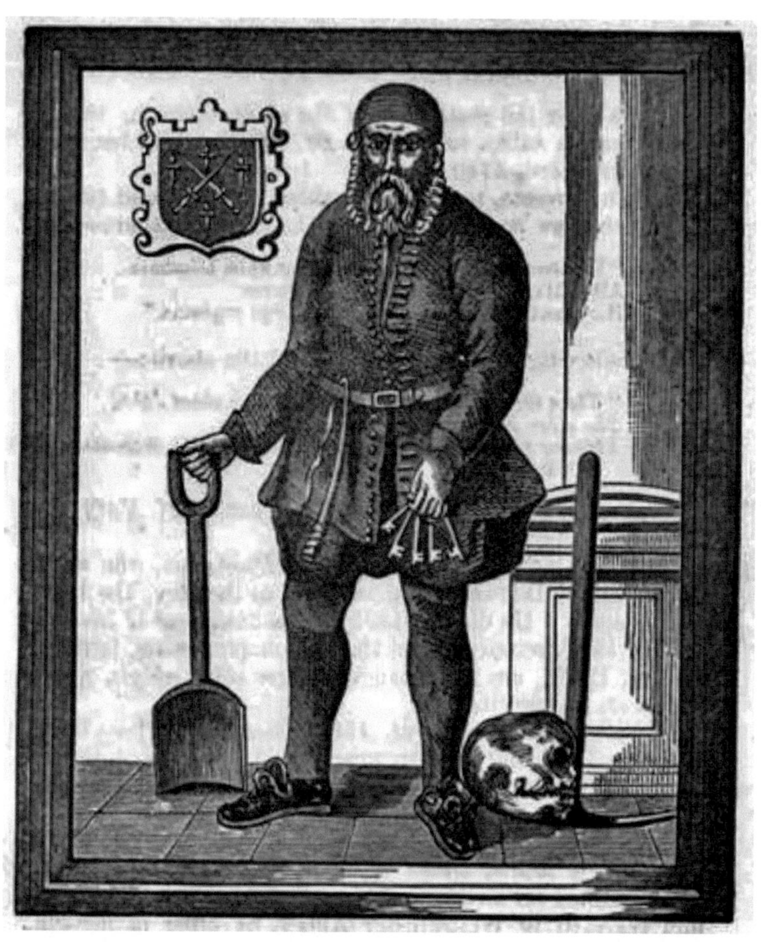

YOV SEE OLD SCARLEITS PICTVRE STAND ON HIE BVT AT YOVR FEETE THERE DOTH HIS BODY LYE HIS GRAVESTONE DOTH HIS AGE AND DEATH TIME SHOW HIS OFFICE BY THEIS TOKENS YOV MAY KNOW SECOND TO NONE FOR STRENGTH AND STVRDYE LIMM A SCAREBABE MIGHTY VOICE WITH VISAGE GRIM HEE HAD INTERD TWO QVEENES WITHIN THIS PLACE AND THIS TOWNES HOVSE HOLDERS IN HIS LIVES SPACE TWICE OVER: BVT AT LENGTH HIS OWN TVRN CAME WHAT HEE FOR OTHERS DID FOR HIM THE

SAME WAS DONE: NO DOVBT HIS SOVL DOTH LIVE FOR AYE IN HEAVEN: THO HERE HIS BODY CLAD IN CLAY.

As you enter the south aisle of the choir, upon the wall is a neat marble tablet to the *Rev. Dr. William Parker*, who died October 3rd, 1730.

Next, in a recess, is a tablet to abbot *Andreas*, and two of his predecessors, with the following Latin inscription: —

"Hos tres abbates quibus est prior abba Iohannes

Alter Martinus, Andreas ultimus unus

Hic claudit tumulus; pro clausis ergo rogemus."

The following is a free translation of the above: —

"These three abbots, of whom the first is abbot John,

The other Martin, the last Andrew,

This one tomb shuts up [incloses]; therefore for those shut up, let us pray."

Above this is a small tablet to the memory of *Mary*, the wife of the *Rev. Payne Edmunds*.

Next, is a marble tablet to *Robert Pemberton*, who was a magistrate of this city, and steward to the Rev. the Dean and Chapter. He died in 1695, in the 75th year of his age.

Near these, removed from the old chapter-house, founded by king Peada, are the statues of *three other abbots*, whose names are unknown.

Adjoining, is an effigy of *Abbot Alexander*, whose body, with his boots and crosier, were found by some workmen when making a foundation for the new choir in 1830, as related at page 15 of this work.

Opposite to this, is a black marble slab, beneath which the body of *Mary, Queen of Scots*, was at first deposited, and remained for twenty-five years, when it was disinterred and removed to Westminster Abbey, by order of her son, king James the 1st. Hanging near it is the original letter of the king ordering the removal. See note on page 29.

At the end of this aisle are two handsome compartments; the left hand, to the memory of *Joseph Stamford*, who died in 1683; and the right hand, to *Thomas Whitwell*, who died at Wisbech in 1759.

Above that of *Joseph Stamford*, is a tablet to *Francis Lockier*, who died 1740; and below, a small tablet to *John Speechley*, for 33 years organist of the cathedral.

We now enter the building known by the name of

The New Building.

"The whole appearance of the interior of this beautiful building is grand and imposing in the extreme; its roof, which is composed of the elaborate fan vaulting, for which the Perpendicular style is so famous, rises from slender shafts, and is ornamented with large and handsome bosses, upon each of which is carved a shield, with armorial bearings. In these respects, as well as in the general aspect of its details, this building so nearly resembles the noble chapel of King's College, Cambridge, as to warrant the supposition that they were both erected from the designs of one architect. The New Building is lighted by thirteen very fine windows, two of which are filled with modern painted glass. The space below the windows is occupied by a rich cornice, an elegant arcade, and a stone seat. Here is to be seen a monument, till lately supposed to be that of abbot Hedda and his monks, whose massacre by the Danes was spoken of in the first chapter of this work, which is considered to be one of the oldest christian monuments now extant in England." See note on page 4.

At the south end of this building, are the remains of a beautiful marble monument, erected by Sir Humphrey Orme, the destruction of which is recorded at page 34 of this work.

By the side of this monument are two tablets, one in memory of *Archdeacon Davys*, his wife *Selina*, and their son *John William Owen*; underneath which is a black tablet, surmounted by a shield, bearing a coat of arms, with a mitre, in memory of *Francis Jeune, D.C.L.,* twenty-fifth bishop of Peterborough, who died in 1868.

On the south-east side of the altar, is a very stately and handsome marble monument of the Corinthian order; on which is a portraiture of the gentleman for whom it was erected, lying on his left side, and leaning on a cushion, with his hand upon a scull; above which statue is this inscription —

"Sacred to the memory of *Thomas Deacon*, Esq., a native of this city; sometime high sheriff of this county: a person eminent for his morality and good life; a true son of the established church: a constant attendant on her worship and service: his piety consisted not in empty profession, but in sincerity and unaffected truth. He had an ample estate, which he fairly acquired, and increased by an honest industry, and managed with excellent prudence, and disposed of to laudable purposes. His charity (even in the time of his life) was very large, extensive, and exemplary; of which he has left a lasting monument in this city, by founding a charity school, and endowing it with a freehold estate, of above one hundred and sixty pounds per annum: And also, by settling another estate of twenty-five pounds per annum, for a constant annual distribution of alms to poor ancient inhabitants of this city. Having thus laid up in store to himself a good foundation against the time to come, he quietly departed this life, on the 19th day of August, 1721, aged 70 years.

"To whose memory as an instance of her conjugal affection, Mary, his sorrowful relict, caused this monument to be erected."

Beneath his effigy, and upon the front of the tomb, is the following inscription —

"In memory of *Mary*, the relict of Thomas Deacon, Esq.; daughter of John Harvey, of Spalding, gent. To which place she was a kind generous benefactor, and bestowed upwards of £400 in pious and useful charities. She gave also to Fleet £250, for founding a charity school in that parish. To the poor of this city, she extended her daily bounty, so private as not to be told; so large as not to be equalled; to which she added several public benefactions, and gave towards augmenting the vicarage of St. John Baptist £100; and likewise £100 to the salary of the grammar school; she died January 27th, 1730, aged 77 years."

In a recess adjoining this monument, is a neat tablet to the memory of *Mary*, the mother of the Rev. J. S. Pratt, formerly a prebendary of this cathedral, and vicar of the parish of St. John the Baptist, Peterborough.

Underneath this, a handsome tablet to the late *William Strong, D.D.*, forty-five years archdeacon of this diocese, and for nearly half a century a magistrate for the Liberty of Peterborough.

Near the last monument, behind the altar screen, are interred the remains of six bishops, viz.:—*Cumberland, Kennett, Hinchcliffe, Madan, Marsh and Davys*; tablets to the four latter, are in the recess opposite the large painted window.

Beneath these, is an effigy, supposed to be that of *Abbot William de Hotot*, who died in 1250.

On the north-east side of the altar, is a very handsome marble monument to *Bishop Cumberland*, great grandfather to the celebrated dramatist of that name.

Beneath this, is a neat tablet to *Joseph Parsons*, formerly a prebendary of this cathedral, and *Letitia*, his wife; near which, is a monument erected to his intimate friend *William Tournay*, D.D., also a prebendary of this cathedral, and of St. Peter's, Westminster, and for twenty-five years warden of Wadham College, Oxford, &c.

Adjoining, are the remains of an ancient shrine, supposed to be that of *St. Ibba*.

Above this is a marble tablet to *Louisa Cole*, of the Vineyard.

On leaving the Lady Chapel, in the north aisle of the choir, is a splendid monument to *Richard Trice*, beneath which is a handsome double *piscina*.

Opposite to this, a small marble monument to *Frances*, wife of *Dean Cosin*, who died March 25th, 1642; above which is an epitaph to *Dorothy*, the wife of *Francis Standish*, formerly precentor of this cathedral, who died in 1689.

Opposite, is another plain black marble slab, similar to that in the south aisle, with a small brass inscription which marks the grave of *Catherine of Arragon*.

On the north wall of the side aisle is a monument by the celebrated Gibbons, with the following inscription—

"Sacred to the memory of *Constance*, daughter of *John May*, of Rawmeare, in Sussex, Esquire; and of *Constance*, his wife, one of the daughters and co-heiress of *Thomas Panton*, of Westminster, knight and baronet, and wife of *John Workman*, prebendary of this church, who, having by all christian virtues and good qualities, been an ornament to her worthy family, and an honour to all her relations in her life, resigned up her soul to God with admirable patience at her death; she deceased in childbed at London; and, together with her infant son, she was according to her desire, here interred, where she had frequently worshipped God, in hope of a joyful resurrection, September 30th, A.D. 1681."

Next, is a tablet to *James Duport*, formerly dean of this cathedral, chaplain to Charles II., and professor of Greek at Trinity College, Cambridge.

Adjoining, is another tablet to the memory of the *Rev. John Workman*, M.A., formerly a prebendary of this cathedral, and rector of Peakirk, &c.

Next, is a tablet to *William Rowles*, of Washingley, and *Ann Wilkinson*, his daughter.

The next is to the *Rev. William Gery*, also a prebendary of this cathedral, and Susannah, his wife, who lived together 47 years. This is a very handsome tablet.

The last is a handsome tablet to the *Rev. William Waring*, A.M., formerly master of the grammar school, who died 1726, aged 66.

In a small chapel, known as the Morning Chapel, dedicated to St. John and St. James, is some *ancient tapestry*; one piece representing St. Peter and St. John healing the lame man at the beautiful gate of the temple; the other representing St. Peter's deliverance from prison. In the north-east corner is a tablet to the *Rev. John Stevens*, A.M., rector of Folksworth, Hunts.; and in the centre of the east wall is a stained glass window, representing four scenes from the life of our Lord. Here also are the remains of the woodwork of the *old choir*, which have been converted into seats, and will serve to show to the curious its former character and style.

The Organ,

which is placed above the screen, dividing the nave from the choir, is a very fine toned instrument, and was built in 1809, by the late Mr. Allen, of Sutton Street, Soho. It has within the last few years been much improved and enlarged. It contains forty-eight stops, viz.:—twelve in the great organ, twelve in the swell, ten in the choir, eight in the pedal organ, and six couplers. These improvements were made by H. P. Gates, Esq., of the Vineyard, and are commemorated by a brass plate on the south side of the organ, inscribed as follows: "To the praise and glory of God and memory of John and Frances Gates, this organ was re-built and enlarged at the charge of Henry Pearson Gates, their son, Anno Domini 1871." The case of the instrument, which is of carved oak, presents towards the nave, a front in the early English style, while on the side looking into the choir, the fronts are decorated, to harmonize with the interior fittings.

The Choir.

As we enter the choir, the bishop's throne, with the stalls, pulpit, pews, and altar screen burst upon us, all of which are beautifully carved. The altar screen is composed of a soft white stone, found near Cambridge; the rest that we have mentioned, is oak, very finely carved in the decorated style of architecture. The bishop's throne especially, with its ogee canopies, and elegant and almost fairy-like spire, rivets the eye of the spectator. The *coup d'œil* of the choir is so strikingly beautiful, from the good arrangement and entire keeping of the whole, that it can scarcely be surpassed.

At the east end, immediately under the large window, are three tablets with the names of all the Abbots, Bishops, and Deans from the foundation of the monastery to the present time, of which the following is a copy:—

List of the Abbots of the Cathedral,
With the date of their appointment.

Saxulphus	654	Acharius	1200

Cuthbaldus	673	Robert of Lindsay	1214
Egbaldus		Alexander	1222
Pusa		Martin of Ramsey	1226
Beonna		Walter St. Edmonds	1233
Celredus		William Hotot	1246
Hedda	833	Iohn de Caleto	1249
Adulphus	972	Robert Sutton	1262
Kenulphus	992	Richard of London	1274
Elsinus	1005	William of Woodford	1295
Arwinus	1055	Godfrey of Croyland	1299
Leofricus	1063	Adam Boothby	1321
Brando	1066	Henry Morcot	1338
Thoroldus	1069	Robert Ramsey	1346
Godricus	1098	Henry of Overton	1361
Matthias	1103	Nicholaus	1391
Ernulpus	1107	Willielmus Genge	1396
Iohn of Salisbury	1114	Johannes Deeping	1408
Henricus de Angeli	1128	Richard Ashton	1438
Martinus de Vecti	1133	William Ramsey	1471
William de Waterville	1155	Robert Kirton	1496
Benedictus	1177	Iohn Chambers	1528
Andreas	1194		

Iohn Chambers was the last Abbot and the first Bishop.

List of the Bishops of Peterborough,
With the date of their appointment.

Iohn Chambers, b.d.	1541	Richard Cumberland, d.d.	1691
David Pool, ll.d.	1556	White Kennet, d.d.	1718
Edmund Scambler, d.d.	1560	Robert Clavering, d.d.	1728
Richard Howland, d.d.	1584	Iohn Thomas, d.d.	1747
Thomas Dove, a.m.	1600	Richard Terrick, d.d.	1757
William Pierse, d.d.	1630	Robert Lamb, ll.d.	1764
Augustine Lindsel, d.d.	1632	Iohn Hinchliffe, d.d.	1769
Francis Dee, d.d.	1634	Spencer Madan, d.d.	1794
Iohn Towers, d.d.	1638	John Parsons, d.d.	1813
Benjamin Lany, d.d.	1660	Herbert Marsh, d.d.	1819
Joseph Henshaw, d.d.	1663	George Davys, d.d.	1839

William Loyd, d.d.	1679	Francis Jeune, d.c.l.	1864
Thomas White, d.d.	1685	William Connor Magee, d.d.	1868

Bishop Davys was advanced to this see in 1839. He was formerly a fellow of Christ's Church College, Cambridge, and took a wrangler's degree in 1803. He subsequently became curate of Littlebury, and in 1814 of Chesterford; this latter curacy he held until Dr. Bloomfield, the late bishop of London, was presented to that living, when Mr. Davys became curate of Swaffham Prior; he afterwards removed to Kensington, and was appointed tutor to the Princess Victoria. Shortly after this he was presented to the rectory of All-Hallows, London, and in 1831 to the deanery of Chester, on which occasion he took the degree of doctor of divinity. He discharged his episcopal duties for a period of about twenty-five years in such a manner as to gain universal esteem; and died at Peterborough, after a short illness, in the 84th year of his age, on the 18th April, 1864.

The Rev. Dr. Francis Jeune, who was appointed to the Bishopric in the room of Dr. Davys, was educated at Pembroke College, Oxford, were he graduated in 1827, when he took a first-class in classics. In 1832 he was admitted into Holy Orders by Dr. Bagot, Bishop of Oxford, being then tutor of his College. In 1834 he was elected to the Head Mastership of King Edward's School, Birmingham, and held that appointment until 1838, when he was nominated to the Deanery of Jersey, and the Rectory of St. Heliers. In 1843 he was elected to the Mastership of Pembroke College, with a canonry at Gloucester annexed, and almost immediately afterwards he was presented by the Dean and Chapter of Gloucester to the Rectory of Taynton. In 1850 he was appointed one of Her Majesty's Commissioners of Inquiry for the University of Oxford, and in 1859 was elected Vice-Chancellor of the University. About three months previous to his promotion to this Bishopric, Dr. Jeune was made Dean of Lincoln, in the room of the Rev. Thomas Garnier. Dr. Jeune lived only four years after his appointment to the see. Suffering from an internal disease he went to Whitby for change of air, where he died on the 21st of August, 1868, after a short and painful illness, and was succeeded by the Rev. W. Connor Magee.

Bishop Magee was born at Cork in the year 1821, his father at that time holding a cure in that city before being presented to the living of St. Peter's, Drogheda, in 1829. His grandfather filled the Metropolitan see of Dublin previous to Archbishop Whately. The future bishop of Peterborough received his earliest education at Kilkenny, from which place, at the age of thirteen, he was removed to Trinity College, Dublin. Here he obtained a scholarship in 1838, and Archbishop King's Divinity prize. He graduated A.B. in 1842, A.M. and B.D. in 1854, and D.D. in 1860. In 1844 Mr. Magee received deacon's orders at the hands of the Bishop of Chester, and in the following year was ordained priest by the Bishop of Tuam. His first curacy was that of St. Thomas, Dublin, which he was obliged to resign through ill health, and after a two years' residence abroad he accepted a curacy at St. Saviour's, Bath, in 1848. Two years later he was appointed to the joint incumbency of the Octagon Chapel, Bath. During his residence in Bath, Mr. Magee published two volumes of sermons. In 1859 he was nominated an Hon. Canon of Wells Cathedral, and received the degree of D.D. from his University; and on the resignation of Dr. Goulburn, minister of Quebec Chapel, Portman Square, London, Canon Magee was appointed to the vacant post. In 1860 he was transferred to the precentorship of Clogher in conjunction with the rectory of Enniskillen; in 1864, on the death of Dr. Newman, he was installed Dean of Cork; and in 1866 was appointed Dean of the Chapel Royal, Dublin. He was enthroned as Bishop of Peterborough shortly after the death of Bishop Jeune in 1868, receiving his appointment from the Conservative Prime Minister, Mr. Disraeli.

List of the Deans of Peterborough,
With the date of their appointment.

Francis Abree, d.d.	1541	Richard Kidder, d.d.	1689
Gerard Carlton, b.d.	1543	Samuel Freeman, d.d.	1691
James Curtop, a.m.	1551	White Kennet, d.d.	1707
Iohn Boxhall, ll.d.	1558	Richard Reynolds, ll.d.	1718
William Latimer, d.d.	1560	William Gee, d.d.	1721
Richard Fletcher, d.d.	1585	Iohn Mandevil, d.d.	1722
Thomas Nevil, d.d.	1590	Francis Lockyer, d.d.	1725
Iohn Palmer, d.d.	1598	Iohn Thomas, d.d.	1740

Richard Cleyton, d.d.	1608	Robert Lamb, ll.d.	1744
George Meriton, d.d.	1612	Charles Tarrant, d.d.	1764
Henry Beaumont, d.d.	1616	Charles M. Sutton, d.d.	1791
William Pierse, d.d.	1622	Peter Peckard, d.d.	1792
Iohn Towers, d.d.	1630	Thomas Kipling, d.d.	1797
Thomas Jackson, d.d.	1638	James Henry Monk, d.d.	1822
Iohn Cosin, d.d.	1640	Thomas Turton, d.d.	1830
Edward Rainbow, d.d.	1660	George Butler, d.d.	1842
James Duport, d.d.	1664	Augustus P. Saunders, d.d.	1853
Simon Patrick	1679	J. J. Stewart Perowne, d.d.	1878

The present Dean of Peterborough, The Very Rev. John James Stewart Perowne, D.D., was born about the year 1823, and married in 1862 Anna Maria, third daughter of the late Humphry William Woolrych, Esq., Serjeant-at-Law, of Croxley, Hertfordshire. His family is of French (Huguenot) extraction, which came over to this country at the Revocation of the Edict of Nantes. He was appointed to the Deanery in August, 1878. He was educated at Norwich Grammar School and at Corpus Christi College, Cambridge, of which College he became a Fellow. He was a Bell's University Scholar in 1842, took the Members' Prize for a Latin Essay on three different occasions, viz., 1844, 1846, and 1847, and graduated B.A. in 1845, in which year he was also Crosse Scholar, and in 1848 he proceeded M.A. and was Tyrwhitt's Hebrew Scholar. Eight years afterwards he took the degree of B.D., having in the meantime been ordained deacon in 1847 and priest in the same year that he took his master's degree. In 1855 he was appointed examining chaplain to the Bishop of Norwich, and was made prebendary of S. Andrew's and canon of Llandaff cathedral in 1869. In 1872 he became prælector in Theology of Trinity College, Cambridge, and in 1873 took his degree of D.D., and became Fellow of Trinity College. In 1875 Her Majesty was pleased to graciously appoint him one of her hon. chaplains, and in the same year he was appointed Hulsean Professor of Divinity. In 1851 and 1852 he was examiner for the Classical Tripos at Cambridge, and select preacher before the University on several different occasions. For 10 years he held the vice-principalship of St. David's College, Lampeter, which appointment he resigned in 1872. Before this, he had been Lecturer in Divinity at

King's College, London, and assistant preacher at Lincoln's Inn. In 1868 he was Hulsean Lecturer, and Lady Margaret's Preacher in 1874-5. From 1867 to 1872 he was third cursal prebendary of S. David's Cathedral. From 1874 to 1876 he was one of the Whitehall preachers. The Dean is the author of "The Book of Psalms, a New Translation with Notes, Critical and Exegetical;" Hulsean Lectures on "Immortality"; a volume of Sermons; occasional Sermons; Articles in Dr. Smith's Dictionary of the Bible; *Contemporary Review; Good Words, &c.* And he is a member of the Company engaged on the revision of the Old Testament.

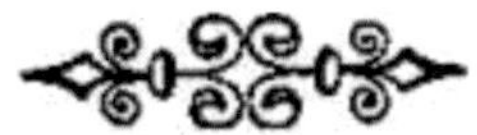

GEO. C. CASTER, PRINTER, MARKET-PLACE, PETERBOROUGH.

PUBLISHED BY
GEO. C. CASTER, Printer & Bookseller,
MARKET PLACE, PETERBOROUGH.

FASTING. A Lenten Sermon, by the Very Rev. J. J. Stewart Perowne, D.D., Dean of Peterborough. Price 3d.

NATIONAL EDUCATION. A Sermon by the Very Rev. J. J. Stewart Perowne, D.D. Price 3d.

OUR DEBT TO THE PAST. Two Sermons by the Rev. Brooke Foss Westcott, D.D., Canon of Peterborough. Price 6d.

ADVENT SERMONS, Preached in Peterborough Cathedral: "The Gospel Preached to the Poor," by the Very Rev. J. J. Stewart Perowne, D.D., Dean; "The Word of God," by the Rev. B. F. L. Blunt, M.A., Vicar of Scarborough; and "Preparation," by the Rev. F. W. Farrar, D.D., Canon of Westminster. 6d. each, by post 7d.; or the three in wrapper, 1/-, by post 1/1.

PETERBOROUGH CATHEDRAL. A General, Architectural, and Monastic History. By Thomas Craddock. Fcap. fo., 234 pages, fancy wrapper, 2/6, cloth gilt, 5/-

NEW GUIDE TO PETERBOROUGH CATHEDRAL. By G. S. Phillips. Illustrated, Crown 8vo., 1/-

PETERBOROUGH CATHEDRAL at the Commonwealth; being extracts from Simon Gunton's History, with a sketch of his life. The work is illustrated by four photographs from scarce engravings, showing the original Ladye Chapel, Altar Screen, etc. Crown 4to., bevelled boards, red edges, 6/-

NOTES ON THE PARISH CHURCHES in and around Peterborough, including the Cathedral, and Crowland, Ramsey, and Thorney Abbeys. By the Rev. W. D. Sweeting, M.A., Head Master of the King's School, Peterborough, Illustrated by 32 Photographs. Demy 8vo., cloth antique, bevelled boards, 21/-; or in three parts, wrappered, 2/6 each.

NOTES ON TWENTY PARISH CHURCHES in the five mile circle round Peterborough, comprising Alwalton, Castor, Eye, Farcet,

Fletton, Glinton, Helpstone, Marholm, Orton Longueville, Orton Waterville, Paston, Peakirk, Stanground, Thorpe, Waternewton, Werrington, Whittlesey (St. Mary), Whittlesey (St. Andrew), Woodstone, and Yaxley. Paper covers, 1/-; cloth, 1/6.

FIRST WORDS AND LAST, or EASTER THOUGHTS, in verse. By Rev. A. S. Newman, M.A. Crown 8vo., paper covers, 1/6; cloth gilt, 2/-

CROWLAND AND THORNEY ABBEYS. By the Rev. W D. Sweeting, M.A., with two photographs, wrappered, 1/-

WILD FLOWERS. Being a list of varieties found in the neighbourhood of Peterborough. By F. A. Paley, M.A. Price 1/-

CÆSAR'S COMMENTARIES. For the use of Junior Classes, Book II., with vocabulary. Price 6d.

CANTICLES POINTED FOR CHANTING. Suitable for Village Choirs. By John Speechley, late Organist of Peterborough Cathedral. Price 1d.

SAVIGAR'S ARITHMETICAL TABLES. For the use of Schools, with rules for mental accounts. Price 1d.; or twelve copies, post free, 1/-

THE SHOWER OF PEARLS. By Charlotte Phillips. A collection of Poems suitable for Home and School use. 14th edition, Demy 18mo., cloth gilt, 1/-

THE BOOK OF ANTHEMS. As used in Peterboro' Cathedral, with a new appendix. Crown 8vo.,

- Cloth lettered on side, red edges2/6
- Ditto, bevelled boards3/-
- Roan, lettered on side, red edges, burnished3/6
- French Morocco limp, gilt or red edges5/-
- Persian limp, gilt or red edges6/-
- Best Calf limp, gilt or red edges7/-
- Best Turkey Morocco do.7/6

PHOTOGRAPHS OF PETERBOROUGH CATHEDRAL. In various sizes, at 6d., 1/-, 2/6, and 5/-

PHOTOGRAPHS OF THE CHURCHES in Sweeting's "Notes on Parish Churches." Carte de Visite size, 6d. each.

DIRECTORY OF PETERBOROUGH and 52 Neighbouring Places, with Plan of the City. Price 2/6.

SPIRIT STOCK BOOKS. 1/- each.

OVERSEER'S and SURVEYOR'S BOOKS and FORMS.

NOTICES TO QUIT. Tenant to Landlord or Landlord to Tenant. 1d. each.

CERTIFICATE FORMS for Baptism, Burial, Banns of Marriage, and Marriage. 1d. each; two dozen, assorted, 1/6.

DISTRAINT NOTICES. 1d. each.

PROBATE FORMS. BANKRUPTCY FORMS.

PARCELS DELIVERY BOOKS. Strongly bound. 100 pages, 2/6; 200 pages, 3/6.

CASTER'S HOUSEKEEPER'S ACCOUNT BOOK. To commence at any time, and last one year. Price 2/-

CONFIRMATION CARDS. In red and black. 1d. each; 25 for 1/6.

AGREEMENT FORMS. For letting Unfurnished Apartments.

RECEIPT BOOKS.

MAP OF PETERBOROUGH, and 20 miles around. Plain, 1/-; Coloured, 1/6; Mounted on Cloth in case, 4/-; Mounted on Roller and varnished, 5/-.

AN APPEAL.

The Dean and Chapter *earnestly hope that Visitors to the Cathedral will contribute something to the Fund in aid of its Restoration. For this purpose a box has been placed in the Nave, under the Screen, and a book in which names, together with the amount of the donation, may be entered. It will be seen that the need of Restoration is urgent, the central tower being much shattered, and its south-eastern pier presenting a very unsightly appearance. One of the most striking features of the Cathedral, the beautiful groined roof of this tower is at present entirely concealed by a scaffold-*

ing put up some years ago when the work of Restoration was suspended for want of funds.

The Dean and Chapter *feel that they may with the more confidence appeal to the liberality of Visitors in aid of the Restoration, because the Cathedral is open free of all charge throughout the day (except during the hours of Divine Service), the Vergers not being allowed to ask for any gratuity.*

Footnotes

1 (Return)
The most probable etymology of this word is that which is given by
Britton in his History of Peterborough Cathedral, viz. — "*Mede* or
Mead, a meadow; *ham*, a sheltered habitation; and *sted, stead*, or *stad*,
a bank, station, or place of rest."
2 (Return)
In cleaning out the river, a little below the bridge, in June, 1820, a
dagger was found, which is supposed to have belonged to these
Danes. It is in the possession of the present Bishop.
3 (Return)
At a meeting of the Archæological Society at Peterborough, in 1861,
Mr. Bloxam read a paper in which he denied the authenticity of this
monument, which had previously been regarded as one of the oldest monumental stones extant. Mr. Bloxam regards it as a Norman,
and not a Saxon work, and some centuries later in date than the
massacre of the monks. He considers that the figures are not mar-
tyred monks with their abbot, but Christ and his eleven disciples. It
has been further conjectured by Canon Westcott that it is part of the
shrine erected over the relics of St. Kyneburgha, which were removed from Castor to Peterborough during the Abbacy of Elsinus,
A.D. 1005-1055. A fragment of sculpture in the same style is built
into the west wall of the South Transept.
4 (Return)
A Saxon King of Northumbria and the second Christian monarch of
that province. An interesting account of this prince, and of the extraordinary miracles said to have been performed by his remains
after death, will be found in a larger edition of the Guide to the
Cathedral, by Thos. Craddock, Esq. Price 2.6 & 15.
5 (Return)
Britton says, on the authority of Gunton, that they sent the secretary
of the monastery over to Denmark, on purpose to obtain it. It is,
however, more probable that Hereward, knowing the disposition of
the Norman abbot would lead him to enrich himself at the expense
of the monastery, took this means of removing temptation out of the
way of Thorold, and subsequently restored the treasure to the monastery, when there was no longer any danger of its being appropriated by the abbot.

6 (Return)
Toot is an old Saxon word, signifying to stand out, or be prominent.
7 (Return)
This sum made the church dependent upon the monastery, and the chaplain was required to bring his church key to the sacrist of the monastery, yearly, as an acknowledgement of it. — *See Gunton's Hist. Church, Peterborough, p. 24.*
8 (Return)
Britton says "he founded a chapel to St. Nicholas *near* it;" but Gunton is doubtless correct, when he says that the chapel was over it.
9 (Return)
After Acharius had recovered the marsh of Singlesholt from the Abbot of Crowland by the law of the land, he let it to him with the understanding that, instead of his paying four stones of wax to the Abbot of Crowland, the abbot should pay him a yearly rental in kind, of the same amount.
10 (Return)
These decrees were, that all churches not consecrated with holy oil, should be dedicated within two years. — *See Britton's Hist. Cathedral Church, Peterborough, pp. 22-3.*
11 (Return)
There was at one time an entrance from the Choir into the Lady Chapel through a door, on the right side of which was a small oratory, with a stone roof; the remains are yet to be seen.
12 (Return)
This hospital was afterwards called Spittle, and some of the stones are still remaining in Spittle-field. It was left by Agnes Pudding, with eight acres of arable land adjoining it.
13 (Return)
The Prince at first refused the robe offered to him, because the abbot did not make a similar offer to his companion; Godfrey, however, soon settled the affair, by presenting one to each.
14 (Return)
A gentleman in this city who is an excellent antiquarian, and has seen the corrody alluded to above, says, "It was granted by charter of the abbot, and presents many curiosities — mentioning particularly the abbot's wine cellar at the over end of the cloister, under the present passage into the square." — *Private MS.*

15 (Return)

The abbot was indicted at the sessions at *Peterburgh* before Guy Woolston. — *Private MS.*

16 (Return)

It is still commonly, but incorrectly, called The Lady Chapel. A building of corresponding position at Lincoln is called the Presbytry.

17 (Return)

Sir William Fitzwilliam, of Milton, to whom the castle then belonged, used to pay visits to the queen of Scots during her confinement, and his noble and gentlemanly conduct, secured the good esteem of Mary. At a later period, a little before the queen was executed, she presented him with a picture of her son, as a testimony of the value which she set upon his friendship. This picture is now in the possession of the Fitzwilliam family.

18 (Return)

The original letter, in the king's own hand-writing, is still in the possession of the Dean and Chapter of Peterborough, and has recently been placed in a frame by the entrance from the south aisle. The following is a copy: — "James R. Trusty and wel-beloved, wee greet you well, for that wee remember it appertaynes to ye duty wee owe to our dearest mother that like honour should be done to hir body and like monument be extant of hir as to others, hirs and our progenitors have bene used to be done, and ourselves have already performed to our deare sister ye late Queen Elizabeth. Wee have commanded a Memoriall of hir to be made in our church of Westminster, ye place where ye Kings and Queens of this realme are usually interred. And for that wee thinke it inconvenient that ye monument and hir body should be in severall places, we have ordered that hir said body remayning now interred in that our Cathedrall Church of Peterborough shalbe removed to Westminster to hir said monument; and have committed ye care and chardg of ye said translation of hir body from Peterborough to Westminster to ye reverend father in God our right trusty and wel beloved servant ye Bishop of Coventry and Lichfield, bearer hereof, to whom wee require you (or to such as ye shall assigne) to deliver ye corps of our said deceased mother, ye same being taken up in a decent and respectfull manner as is fitting. And for that there is a pall now upon ye hearse over hir grave which wilbe requisite to be used to cover hir said body in ye removing thereof, which may perhapps be deemed as a ffee that should belong to ye church. We have appointed ye said reverend father to pay you a reasonable redemption for ye same, which being done by him wee require you that he may have ye pall to be used for ye purpose aforesaid. Given under our signet at our Honor of Hampton Court ye eight and twentieth day of September in ye tenth yeare of our reigne of England, France and Ireland, and of Scotland ye six and fortieth. To our trusty and welbeloved ye Dean and Chapter of our Cathedrall Church of Peterborough, and in theire absence to ye right reverend father in God ye Bishop of Peterborough and to such of ye Prebends or other officers of that church as shalbe found being there."

19 (Return)

This ancient record is said to have been written about the year 1217, by a monk named Hugh Candidus. It is a MS. account of the History of the Abbey from its foundation. Dean Patrick gives the following account of its singular preservation: — "One book indeed, and but one, still remains, which was happily redeemed from the fire by the then precentor of the church, Mr. Humfrey Austin, who knowing the great value of it, first hid it, in February, 1642, under a seat in the quire: and when it was found by a soldier on the twenty-second of April, 1643 (when all the seats were pulled down), rescued it again by the offer of ten shillings, 'for that old latin bible' as he called it, and about which he pretended to enquire. The name of the bible by the help of the ten shillings, preserved this precious treasure from the flames, whither it was going, as Mr. Austin hath left a record in the beginning of the book; with a copy of the soldier's acknowledgement: — *'This booke was hide in the Church by me Humphrey Austin; February, 1642. And found by one of Coll. Cromwelle souldyers when they pul'd down all the seats in the quire, April 22th, 1643. And I makeing inquirie amongst them for an old Latin Bible which were lost, I found out at last the partie who had it, and I gave him for the booke tenn shillings as you see by this acquittance.... The coppie of his acquittance: — I pray let this Scripture Book alone, for he hath paid me for it, and therefore I would desire you to let it alone. By me Henry Topcliffe, souldyer under Captain Cromwell, Colonel Cromwell's sonn; therefore I pray let it alone. —* By me Henry Topcliffe.'" This Ancient Manuscript book is now kept with other documents in the Chapter house of the Cathedral.

20 (Return)

Dean Patrick, in his supplement to *Gunton's History of the Cathedral*, says it was famous for three things, "a stately front, a curious altar piece, and a beautiful cloister." Mr. Davys, in his *Guide*, also says, "we learn, from other writings, that the stall-work, in its choir, was remarkably fine, that its windows of painted glass were of a most superb description, and that, in the number, and beauty of its monuments and brasses, it excelled most of the other churches of the realm. Its central tower, though then in an incomplete state, was much finer than it now is, as it had a handsome octagon above what now forms the central tower. The north western transept tower was also adorned with a lofty spire. This spire, which was of wood covered with lead, was taken down soon after this time."

21 (Return)

"Wulfade was much addicted to hunting, and one day pursuing a goodly hart, which being hotly pursued, took soil in a fountain near unto the cell of St. Chad, who espying the hart weary, and almost spent, was so compassionate towards him that he covered him with boughs and leaves, conjecturing, as if heaven had some design in the access and deportment of that beast. Presently comes Prince Wulfade, and enquired of St. Chad concerning the hart, who answered, That he was not a keeper of beasts, but the souls of men, and that Wulfade was then, as an hart to the water brooks, sent by God to the fountain of living water: which Wulfade hearing with astonishment, entered into further conference with St. Chad in his cell, and was by him baptized: and returning with joy to his father's court, he secretly told his brother Rufine of all that had passed, perswading him to be baptized also; to which Rufine consenting, Wulfade brought him to St. Chad, who likewise baptized this other brother."

22 (Return)

"This Christian pair of brothers did often resort to a private oratory, where they performed their devotions; but at length being discovered to their father by the steward Werbode, who instigated, and enflamed the fire of paternal fury against the sons, King Wolfere, the father, watching the time when his sons were gone to pray, followed them, and entering the oratory, slew both his sons with his own hand; and he, and Werbode demolishing the place, left the bodies of his sons buried in the rubbish." "Queen Ermenild, having

searched for the bodies of her sons, found them out, and giving them burial, [in one stone coffin,] built in the same place where they were slain, a church of stone."
23 (Return)
Dean Kipling, on the authority of tradition, is of opinion, that St. Chad's well was in the quadrangle on the south side of the minster, called the laurel court; but Gunton says, "St. Chad had his cell in the county of Stafford, was the first bishop of Lichfield, where he founded the cathedral church, and there lieth buried." And this assertion would appear to be born out by the fact that the "church of stone" referred to in the previous note, is known to have been erected at *Stone*, in Staffordshire.
24 (Return)
The present painted windows are of modern date, excepting one or two, which are composed of fragments of the windows of the cloisters above described.
25 (Return)
Gunton says, "that in the foundation thereof, Peada laid such stones, as that eight yoke of oxen could scarce draw one of them."
26 (Return)
See *Britton's His. Cathedral Church of Peterboro'*, note p. 53.
27 (Return)
James Henry Monk, afterwards bishop of Gloucester.
28 (Return)
Garbett's Architectural Account of Peterborough Cathedral.]
29 (Return)
Britton, in speaking of these door-ways, says, "There are also two door-ways to the southern aisle of the nave, *both* having *semicircular* arches, &c.;" but this is evidently an oversight.
30 (Return)
These door-ways are supposed to have been built in the middle of the 12th century. It is worthy of remark, that one door-way in the western wall, which is now filled up, is attributed to the Anglo-Saxon age.
31 (Return)
Vide note at page 4 of this work.
32 (Return)
The columns of the beautiful west front were also composed of the same marble; but, being much dilapidated, they were in the time of

Dean Monk, taken down, the best sorted and again put up, and the others replaced by Ketton stone.